To Don — Best of luck — Be safe!

LESSONS FROM A GANG COP

AF173368

TONY MORENO

Tony "Pacman" [signature]

Printed in the United States of America

Design by Michael C. Chettleburgh

ISBN 0-9733381-0-5

Second Edition

This book is dedicated to the past…father Tony, mother Aurora and sister Gloria. This book is also dedicated to the present…sons Ryan and Marcus, daughters Kimberly and Desiree. And this book is dedicated to the future….grandsons Nolan and Shane, as well as granddaughter Alana.

This book is also dedicated to my brothers and sisters, sworn and civilian, past and present, serving the Los Angeles Police Department and to our extended family of professionals throughout law enforcement.

Finally, this book is dedicated to my fellow members of the Los Angeles Police Department's Gang Field Unit, one of the premiere law enforcement units in the world, proudly and effectively working in the gang world's "eye of the hurricane". I know, because I work there ..

Contents

INTRODUCTION: THINGS HAPPEN IN THREES
By Michael C. Chettleburgh, ... 7

SECTION ONE: COMPETENCE 17
1. Don't Let Others Place a Ceiling on Your Learning 19
2. Prepare Yourself for the Enemy Within 25
3. Don't Get Bitter, Get Better 31
4. Knowledge is a Mountain to Climb 39
5. Cultivate and Project a Four Aces Mentality 46
6. Know the Ocean That Surrounds Your Island 51
7. What Motivates Others Should Be Important To You .. 56
8. Only When You Are in Control Are You Safe 61
9. Follow The Piñata Principle 66

SECTION TWO: CHARACTER 71
10. Being a Character is Not Having Character 73
11. Celebrate Victory With Dignity 79
12. Focus On The "A" For Effort 83
13. What Goes Around, Comes Around 87
14. Develop Their Trust in You 92
15. What A Leader Does 98
16. Manage the Competitive Spirit 105

SECTION THREE: COMMITMENT 113
17. Do Something For Yourself Outside Your Work 115
18. Learn From Your Emotional Baptism 121
19. You Can't Change People, But You Can Influence
     Them 132
20. Develop Your Own Style of Working Gangs 138

21. Acres of Diamonds In Your Backyard 146
22. Dealing With The "We Have No Gangs" Syndrome 152
23. Worry Little About Lack of Community Support 158
24. It Takes a Community 163
25. I Guess I Didn't Need It 172
26. The Most Important Lesson 183

ACKNOWLEDGMENTS 189

INTRODUCTION

Things Happen in Threes

By Michael Chettleburgh

Since ancient times it has been said that "things happen in threes". Numerologists, who look for meaning in numbers, are not alone in believing there is an inherent magic in threes. Trinities have been endowed with meaning since ancient times, and there are examples of triads throughout literature, folklore, religion and even sports.

Trinities of gods existed in Greece, Egypt and Babylon. Throughout Arthurian legend you will find three challenges that had to be met before the quest was completed. Christianity has the Holy Trinity, and the Brothers' Grimm story *Rumpelstiltskin* features many instances where things happen in threes. Even today in modern sports, certain trinities are the paragon of achievement: the triple play in baseball; the Triple Crown in horse racing; and hockey's hat trick.

In my lifetime, there is a series of events that stands out, and it relates to having met three people who, either at the time of our meeting or sometime before that, were among the very best in the world in their respective fields.

In 1982, as a 17-year old hockey player away from home for the first time, I had the pleasure of meeting Wayne Gretzky in his hometown, Brantford, Ontario, Canada. At the time, I was a rookie for the Brantford Alexander's Major Junior "A" Hockey Club in the Ontario Hockey League, playing alongside Wayne's 15-year old younger brother, Keith. For a young hockey player in Canada, competing with many others to try to make it to the NHL, meeting the "Great Gretzky" was the stuff of dreams, especially since only months before he had set a new NHL record of 92 goals in a single season.

Fast forward to 2000. In collaboration with an international magazine, I undertook to write a series of feature articles on leaders in the international financial community. I was fortunate enough to secure a two hour interview with the "Dean of Global Investing" and legendary billionaire philanthropist, Sir John Templeton, in his quiet oak paneled boardroom overlooking the lush Lyford Cay, just outside of Nassau in the Bahamas.

Then in 2002, in Toronto, Canada, I met Tony Moreno of the Los Angeles Police Department, the author of this book and one of the most talented and committed gang cops the world has ever seen.

Knowing Tony as well as I now do, I know he would stridently dispute this characterization as one of the top talents in his field. He would say that there are no gang gurus, as the modern street gang is just too complex an organism. He would disagree with me not because of any lack of confidence in his skills or abilities, or because he undervalues his many career accomplishments. Rather, he respects deeply the skills and contributions of his law enforcement brothers and sisters and the interdependence that is necessary to succeed in their violent world. He would rebuke my characterization because of the inherent challenges that he faces, even today, as a 28-year veteran of the Los Angeles Police Department. And he would debate my characterization because Tony Moreno is just Tony, a humble and honest cop whose spiritual payment comes from the knowledge of a job well done, rather than personal accolades and recognition.

To be sure, Tony will likely never achieve the financial success of Wayne Gretzky or Sir John Templeton but that is, after all, only one measure of a man. The ironic thing, however, is that Tony's attempt to downplay his career achievements only reinforces his similarity to the likes of Gretzky and

8

Templeton and perhaps the vast majority of individuals who have achieved greatness in their respective professions.

While my nerves got the better of me and I said but a few words to Gretzky back in 1982, countless television interviews I saw after that confirmed his modesty, respect for others, his desire to improve and his preoccupation with the contribution of his team. Since I did spend a meaningful amount of time with Sir Templeton, however, I asked him the questions "what do you consider your greatest achievement?" and "what would you like to be remembered for?" It was his response to these questions that was very telling, "I simply do not think in those terms"; a response that stemmed from his most enduring trait - his humility. Despite being almost ninety years old at the time, Sir Templeton was still looking forward rather than looking back; still finding ways to improve the world around him and achieve an even higher level of understanding and spiritual growth.

In a very real way, then, these three leaders are linked by much more than their career achievements. They have professional competence and commitment, but most important, they have character - the inherent attributes that determine a person's moral and ethical actions and reactions.

Tony Moreno was born in 1952 in Los Angeles to Aurora and Anthony Moreno, second generation Mexican-Americans who had settled in Boyle Heights in East L.A. along with Tony's older sister, Gloria.

Situated just east of the Los Angeles River, Boyle Heights has long been a gateway for newcomers to the city. From the 1920s to the 1950s it was Los Angeles' most diverse neighborhood, serving as home to large concentrations of Jews, Mexicans, and Japanese Americans, as well as Russian Molokans, African Americans, and people of Armenian, Italian, and Chinese descent. Boyle Heights was a community in which everyone knew and looked out for each other, a community where people left their doors unlocked at night because they felt just that safe.

Tony's mother was a homemaker, while his dad was a wholesale buyer of construction equipment who supplemented the family's income by cutting lawns in the evenings and on weekends. Like other lower middle class homeowners in the community looking to get ahead, Tony's parents invested heavily in their family, in particular instilling in their children honesty, respect and hard work. Looking back, Tony describes his parents as having had very high expectations of him and his sister, so much so that that the two things the siblings were most afraid of was pissing off Dad, and hurting their mother's feelings. Even early on, Tony knew that he did not want to end up in juvenile hall, where he would then have to explain to his parents - who seldom gave him the benefit of a doubt - what he had done to get there.

Tony recalls that as a young boy, his parents stressed the importance of learning to speak and write well in English, even more so than Spanish, not out of any lack of pride in their Hispanic heritage, but because mastery of these communication skills was considered essential to get ahead in the United States. As a way of teaching Tony how to read and spell in English, Tony's dad gave him football trading cards - if he could read or spell the words on the card, he got to add it to his collection. In 1960, when playing alone in his front yard, a census taker asked to see his parents, who were not home at the time. Intent on doing his job, the census taker began questioning the eight-year old Moreno. When he asked Tony "What nationality are you?", he simply replied with a puzzled look "English!", the language he had come to know as his principal one.

To be sure, life in Boyle Heights was far from perfect. The cultural diversity and economic conditions in the community meant that there was an ebb and flow of tension, including the relationship with the police. There existed a small cadre of

10

gang members in the community who tended to be from broken, immigrant families. Although Tony knew some of these kids, he was taught by his father (who despised gang members) the value of both family and rugged individualism - that you can act as an individual, and that you don't need to be part of a group to succeed in life. By 1964, however, the gang problem had worsened in the community, and the Moreno family moved to a better part of Boyle Heights, due in large part to a gang member having pulled a knife on Tony's dad.

Several years later, Tony graduated from Montebello High School and wondered what he wanted to do for a living. While he had had a couple of negative contacts with the police growing up - not because of anything he had done wrong but because of what he looked like - he was attracted to a police recruitment poster displayed in a junior college. It highlighted the courses that were being offered over the next two years as preparation for police academy. Tony enjoyed televised police dramas like the *Naked City*, which had its heyday between 1958 and 1963, and he respected the job that police officers performed. And perhaps because it was not considered "cool" by his contemporaries to become a cop, this profession intrigued him even more. Even then, doing the things that others did not want to do was part and parcel of Moreno's personality and world view.

Tony enjoyed the two-year's worth of courses, then entered the LAPD academy, a decision that his mother didn't like, but one greeted by his father with the three simple words: "Just do well". Entering the academy, Tony realized just how "Mexican" he was. While in high school it was commonplace for a class to be composed of 40% Hispanics and 60% white kids, the police academy did not exhibit this level of diversity. As if in an attempt to break him, to show that he was not tough enough or worthy of membership in the LAPD, academy supervisors taunted and cajoled him. Tony vividly recalls hand-gun training, where students had to shoot dummies for points - obviously a competitive and stressful experience. The

11

shooting instructor proceeded to issue directions to the class, but singled out Tony before the shooting began: "Moreno, you just run up and stab him in the chest!". Fortunately for the citizens of Los Angeles, he didn't take the comments personally and successfully completed academy.

Tony knew early on in his career that he wanted, if not deserved, to work gangs. In several of his early ride-alongs in troubled South-Central Los Angeles, he felt distinctly at home. He knew that South-Central was among the most dangerous and gang-infested communities in the world, yet intuitively, he felt that it was the environment where he could make his greatest contribution. The community needed him, and he needed the community. He grew up with gang members close by and understood their world; he could "speak their language" and had the instinct for the ever-present life-and-death dynamic of the violent street gang. And he knew that relative to many other young officers who were finding their way in law enforcement, he was more prepared to do the work others did not want to do; not because it would lead to a life of accolades, but because he was meant to be there, to learn, and then to share with others around him.

The rest, as they say, is history, snippets of which are contained within *Lessons From A Gang Cop*.

Lessons From A Gang Cop **is Tony's contribution to his law enforcement brothers and sisters who toil everyday to be safe, productive and effective in what they do.** Unlike other books on the subject, *Lessons From A Gang Cop* does not focus on gangs, their origins or their criminal activities. Rather, the book presents the key principles Tony Moreno believes are essential for the mental, physical and emotional well-being of law enforcement and other front-line professionals dealing with violent gangs and fighting to make our communities safer. It is a product of Tony's 28 years of service on the Los

Angeles Police Department, and perhaps most important, it is an expression of love to his son Ryan who joined the LAPD in 1995. As Tony says, nothing so focused his mind on sharing secrets to success and happiness in policing than seeing his own flesh and blood follow in his footsteps.

In working with Tony over the better part of the last 12 months on this book, it became evident from his writings that three themes, or "factors for success", emerged with respect to a career in law enforcement - competency, character and commitment. Indeed, these three themes are so evident that we use them here as a theoretical framework that divides the book into three component parts: the Three C's of *Lessons From A Gang Cop*. Again confirmation that things happen in threes.

To be successful in policing, as in life, one needs to have a healthy dose of all three characteristics. Perhaps you know of a competent and committed police officer who has all the tools to do his or her job, but suffers from a faulty mindset that breeds mistrust and resentment. Or perhaps you know of a highly ethical and driven police officer, but that person just doesn't have a knack for the technical aspects of what is a very difficult and process-driven job. It is only when one achieves a mastery of all three traits of competence, character and commitment, that true success is achievable.

With Tony Moreno, I have come to know a man who embodies these traits and lives them every day. To be sure, Tony's achievements are worthy of our respect and gratitude, but in reality, he is like most others in the world of law enforcement. Unlike many, though, he has chosen not to be governed by uncertainty and self-doubt; he has chosen to break through barriers and tap his vast potential; he has chosen not to take himself or others too seriously, especially those who, through their words and actions, try to diminish him; and he has chosen to earn his reputation one inch at a time, one street corner at a time, one interview at a time, one arrest at a time.

What he has achieved is available to all of you. In a very real way, the next frontier is not only in front of you, it is *inside of you*. You and all of your police counterparts have vast potential and a remarkable destiny that is just waiting to be lived. So, like Tony Moreno, just choose to live it. You, your family and the community around you will be glad you did.

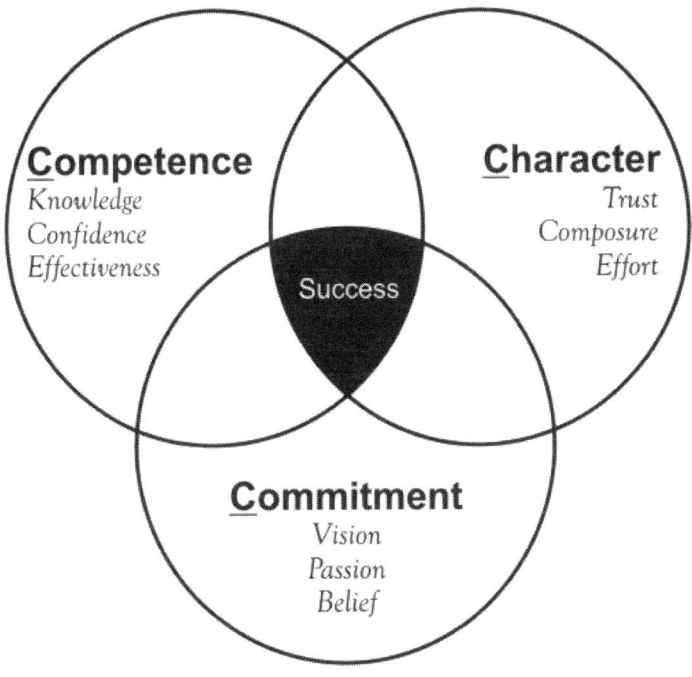

The Three C's of
LESSONS FROM A GANG COP

*In law enforcement, as in life, it is at the intersection of the
Three C's where true success is achievable.*

Competence

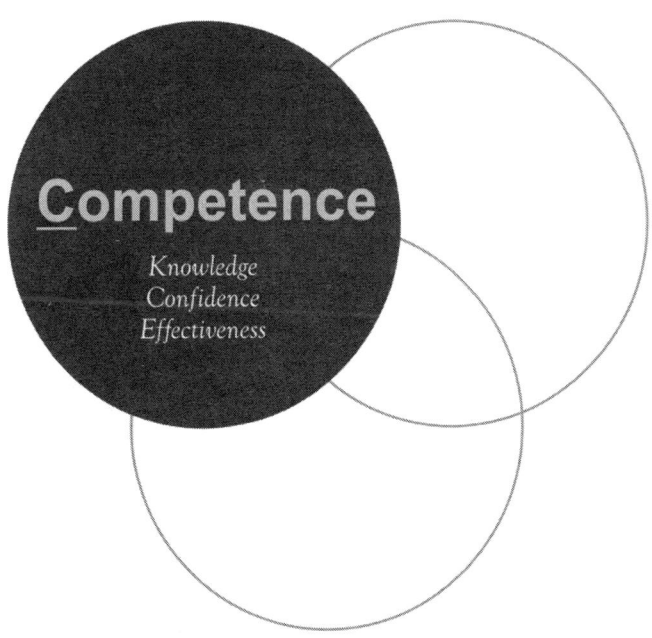

Competence

Knowledge
Confidence
Effectiveness

Don't Let Others Place a Ceiling on Your Learning

Leadership and learning are indispensable to each other.

JOHN F. KENNEDY

As a young officer learning the gang trade, it was commonplace for me to pepper questions to my superiors and other experienced officers about anything and everything to do with gangs. My thirst for knowledge was acute, and I believed that to be safe and effective in my job, I needed to learn as much as possible, as quickly as possible.

For the most part, the law enforcement experts I encountered in the field were helpful. But regularly, I would come across someone who appeared to be threatened by my quest for practical information. To me, it seemed that they wanted to limit how much I should know or learn, almost as if by sharing their insights, their power would somehow be diminished. As a young officer, this phenomenon was quite confounding. Weren't we on the same side of the thin blue line? Weren't we all sworn to enforce the laws of the land and protect our citizens?

Some context is helpful in understanding my predicament. When I graduated from the academy in 1976, I was assigned to Van Nuys Division in the so-called "slower" San Fernando Valley region of Los Angeles. I wasn't particularly happy about being deployed there, because my preference would have been to go to the hectic Newton Street Division in South-Central Los Angeles where I did my ride-alongs while in the academy. I was totally

19

comfortable working in that environment. The people in that area of the city really needed and appreciated the police, and the action was fast and furious.

Back then, a new officer's probationary period in Los Angeles was a total of one year from the day you entered the academy. Since the academy was a total of five months, this meant that you did seven months of probationary time while actually in the field. Since I had the knack and instinct for police work, I did very well on probation. It also helped that I had grown up in East Los Angeles - another community with its share of challenges - because I came to understood people and their problems. As well, being raised in East L.A. instilled in me a sense for trouble and trouble makers.

Because I performed well while on probation, my supervisor decided that I no longer needed to be assigned to a training officer. In a move that would benefit me greatly, I was assigned to an officer with more than 15 years on the job who had been sent to Van Nuys Division a few years earlier in order to "chill out" because, as the story went, he had been involved in so many shootings while working Southwest Division. The Southwest Division was a very active one and to this day, more officers have been killed while on duty there than any other division of the Los Angeles Police Department. Since I hadn't yet met him, I could only form an initial opinion from what I had heard. Most other officers weren't big on the idea of working around him because they were dealing with their own problems and didn't want the added responsibility of calming down an allegedly fast-on-the-draw "gunslinger". It also didn't help that this veteran wasn't a friendly and cuddly person. "Let that rookie Moreno worry about that crap" was the quickest solution to the problem as far as management was concerned. While I accepted my re-assignment with a little unease, I decided to make the most of it. Lucky for me, this guy turned out to be one of the finest, most talented street cops that I've ever been around. I learned so much from him, and to this day feel extremely fortunate to have been his partner, even if it was only for a few short months.

Among the many things that I learned from him, three key lessons in particular helped prepare me to be an effective police officer. First, I learned that in police work you are called upon to take control. When you exert and establish control, only then are you safe. When you get to a crime scene, you must take control. When you encounter danger, you must take control. He told me that a lot of officers didn't understand the importance of taking control or didn't have what it took to exert or establish control. At times, it takes courage, other times, daring. He impressed upon me that if I learned to take control that would mean I had courage - the ability to control fear. To him, being able to take control was the hallmark of a good cop, and that is all he wanted out of me as his partner.

The second lesson that stands out was that everyone encountered should be accorded a certain amount of dignity. Victim, witness, suspect, fellow cop, civilian, janitor or supervisor, it didn't matter, treating them with dignity just made your job easier. But there was an underlying strategy to his way of treating people. Specifically, how a person reacted to my partner's offer of dignity determined how he dealt with that person from that point on. If you acted like a lady or gentleman, you were treated like one. If you acted like a knucklehead, you got treated like one.

He gave away dignity, but he didn't give away any of his strength. If you needed to go to jail and refused, you were going to get your ass kicked if that's what it took. He was secure enough in himself to know that treating people with dignity - regardless of how bad they might have been - didn't make you any less of a man or any less effective as a cop. What was really enlightening for me about this dignity lesson was that even the hardest core gang members respected him. He didn't talk down to them, and that is important to gangsters who crave respect. Gang members know that in the business of being a gangster, they will have to deal with the cops. It makes sense that they'd rather deal with a cop to whom they can relate.

The third lesson was about the importance of investing the time and energy to learn about the people and places around you. My partner didn't speak Spanish, but knew more about a particular Hispanic gang than anyone in the Department. He knew more about that gang because he devoted his time to learning all that he could – the names and nicknames of their members, their hangouts, their allegiances and enemies and their unique ways of communicating. To gain this know-how, he didn't just rely on police experts, but sought the advice of the community and even gang members. If he encountered a roadblock in his search for knowledge, he would simply find another source. He didn't let anyone stop him from learning what he had to learn to be effective. He also encouraged me to learn the gang, which I really tried to do under his guidance. He cared for me and wanted me to know the gang as well as he did. He encouraged my education by sharing all of his vast knowledge, with no strings attached.

A few months later, I got wheeled (a mandatory transfer once you've completed probation) to Newton Street Division. "Shootin' Newton", as it was affectionately called, was a much faster paced Division than Van Nuys, and what I had learned from my ex-partner was invaluable in my new surroundings. Control was my highest priority when doing my job and I quickly gained the respect of my fellow officers even though I came from the "valley". They saw that I wouldn't wait around for someone else to take charge. I took care of business.

I grew up around Hispanic gangs all my life, so I was accustomed to the gang lifestyle and culture. Working Newton Street Division, however, gave me my first contact with Crips and Bloods, violent black street gang members whose numbers ran into the thousands throughout Los Angeles. By giving them dignity and respect, I got repaid with information and trust. It also enabled me to learn and be successful.

It was fortunate that I had such a strong foundation built upon the lessons of my ex-partner, since during my new assignment I began to be exposed to gang "experts" whom, when asked a Blood or Crip gang-related question, would seem reluctant to share information or would provide a rather empty or cryptic response. It didn't take me long to realize that, "Hey, these guys don't want me to know". I called this the local sheriff syndrome - police experts who didn't want outsiders to "mosey into town" to learn on their time and therefore, ultimately know more than they did. The local sheriff was the guy who felt that if I learned more than he knew, he somehow wouldn't be needed anymore or I would somehow diminish his value and reputation. He was the person who didn't want to share information that might enhance my safety, my fellow officers' safety, and the safety of innocent citizens, only because he didn't want me to get too proficient at working gangs.

I decided at this early point in my career that no one was going to stop me from knowing what I needed to know. No one was going to put a ceiling on my learning.

This is a lesson that I have passed to many other police officers, and now hopefully to you. Realize that while the advice and counsel of a true expert can be very valuable, there is always more than one source of information, especially on gangs. You don't always have to squeeze information out of the local sheriff, nor should you feel guilty if you feel compelled to bypass the local gang "authority" (he or she may or may not actually be that qualified in the first place) in favor of an outside resource.

I experience this quite often when dealing with officers from other parts of the country. Because L.A. gangsters travel all over the United States and have spread their influence, I frequently get calls and e-mails from police officers requesting information on certain gangs. Many times, I'll ask why they haven't received gang training, especially when they are inundated with L.A. gangsters. The typical response is, "Well, we have our local expert, but he's pretty useless. He just goes to seminars but we really don't benefit from what he does, but, he's supposedly the man."

As a case in point, I recently had contact with a law enforcement officer from the east coast who didn't want anyone to know that he made contact with me. He was dealing with a gang member with Los Angeles affiliations, and he needed information that related to specific officer safety issues. He told me that it was clear in his mind that if the local District Attorney learned that he contacted an outside expert rather than the local one, his career would be made much tougher. While the District Attorney was enamoured with the so-called local expert, no one else was.

This officer was doing the right thing. He wasn't going to let the local powers-that-be decide how much he was going to learn. Nor should you. If the door isn't open, or if you can't get a reasonable answer, or you don't think the supposed authority can add any value to your work, then find another source of knowledge. They do exist, and many are open to help. Never let anyone put a ceiling on your learning. Your life, and the lives of others, may very well depend on it.

2

Prepare Yourself for the Enemy Within

Failure to prepare is preparing to fail.

UNKNOWN

If you are like most police officers I know, you will probably stay in law enforcement for twenty to thirty years. The sheer magnitude and diversity of experiences you will face in this period of time demands that you keep things in their proper perspective. What this really means is that you can't let your enthusiasm, emotion and passion for the job evaporate due to that enemy within - burnout - especially within your first few years on the job.

This advice applies not only to law enforcement officers, but also to others working in and around the criminal justice field, including attorneys, probation officers, counsellors and even educators. Like police officers, these professionals come into contact with gang members on a regular basis. While the nature of this contact may be different in kind, it usually is not in degree. These professionals, too, are at risk of burning out, and must find a way to endure and succeed, especially when dealing with hardened gang members and relentless gang violence.

Gang work can be an intense, on-going series of investigations, interviews, confrontations, set-backs, successes and disappointments. If you realize what you are getting into and the dangers that lurk, you can better prepare yourself for what's ahead. It's difficult and frustrating work, but it can also be highly rewarding and challenging.

Recently, I received an e-mail from a police officer who works gangs in a medium-sized mid-western U.S. city. He complimented me on my career achievements, but was especially impressed that I had been able to work gangs for over 28 years and not crash and burn. This officer had been working gangs in his city for approximately six months, and was already beginning to feel the siren call of burnout. Try as he might to put his important work into perspective and improve his attitude, he had just about had enough.

What the officer didn't understand is that I, like anyone else who is deeply involved in their work, had suffered from burnout. The difference was that I didn't respond to this phenomenon as if it were a terminal disease. Just because I felt like I was burning out, it didn't mean that I was a failure or that my career had come to an end. It didn't even mean that I had to change my assignment or the nature of my work. To me it was, and still is, a temporary state of mind.

Burnout meant that I was in a place where I was not suitably motivated and had stopped caring as much about my work. Quite simply, I had stopped finding reward in what I was doing. But by knowing myself and how my mind dealt with the good and bad stimuli surrounding gang work, I knew that burnout was essentially going to be a situation of "here today, gone tomorrow".

Life, as in police work, is a series of phases. Your classes and the teachers in school change. Your friends constantly change. Your hairstyle and tastes in music change. Your needs and wants change. Your lovers and your enemies change. Nothing stays the same.

An old-time officer once told me that I could drive down the same street a hundred times and that every time I did so, something would be different. His point was to always be ready and be engaged; that being complacent when driving down that old familiar street the next time might just mean the end of you. He was right. Things do always change. Things evolve, sometimes for the better, sometimes for the worse, but they do change.

A big part of dealing constructively with burnout is to realize that there are some things that you may have no control over. All of us working gangs or deployed on patrol know that despite our best efforts in prevention and suppression, the gang problem is worsening in North America. That is not an indictment of the quality of our work or our collective commitment to our profession, it is simply a reflection of the fact that this problem is a large and complex one that isn't going to be solved overnight. If you focus on your and your peers' relative inability to quickly stem the growth or severity of gang activity in your jurisdiction, you may develop a negative and cynical attitude that's difficult to break. Not only will it affect your performance and others' perception of you at work, it will inevitably spill out into your personal life. The high suicide, divorce and alcoholism rates that pervade the law enforcement field are a testament to the rigors of our work, indeed.

If your chief isn't who you want your chief to be or your supervisor is more concerned with his career than your welfare, deal with it. They probably aren't going to change who they are or how they do what they do. Once you get some perspective of who they are and what they are about, it can save you from being blind-sided and expecting too much. Being disappointed will only bring on frustration and bitterness in your life.

I know officers who complain incessantly about the impact of issues such as immigration or the changes brought about by having more women in their department. Immigration and women are here to say. Deal with it. Do yourself a favor and accept things for what they are. You don't have to like them, but once you figure out that you can't always affect change, you relieve some of the pressure on yourself. As the great American philosopher William James wrote, "Human beings, by changing the inner attitudes of their minds, can change the outer aspects of their lives". You don't have to like change or agree with it, just amend your attitude, accept change, and find a constructive way to deal with it. If you do so, you'll be amazed at how your outlook at work - and in life - will improve.

Don't get me wrong: I know this can sometimes be easier said than done. The present day realities and politics of policing can get you stuck in a deep rut. Your negative frame of reference can build up to the point where you see no end in sight. You begin to question why you chose this career in the first place. You fondly recall that sense of purpose and honor that motivated you to get involved in law enforcement. You reminisce about the feeling you had when you were handed your first badge or when you made your first arrest. You desperately want that feeling again, the feeling of power and purpose, the feeling of being unique because you will do things and dedicate yourself to the point where most people fear to venture.

But if you are to be effective and healthy in this profession, you must find a way, some way, to extricate yourself from feelings of despair. I suggest that you find an emotional trigger - an image, a concept, a previous event, a feeling - something that reminds you of your original sense of purpose and passion for policing and therefore transports you back to a positive state of mind.

My emotional trigger is a single, carefully maintained picture of a four-year old girl who was shot in the head during a drive-by shooting involving some Crip gang members in Los Angeles. This little girl, Tina, was simply in the wrong place at the wrong time. The bullet entered her chin and lodged in her throat, requiring delicate emergency surgery.

The photograph is a compelling one. It is a facial shot of her staring at the camera. You can see the fright, pain and confusion in her eyes. The utter injustice of the entire incident grabs and wrenches me in the gut, and serves to remind me of why I am a police officer.

When I feel tired, burnt out or just plain sorry for myself, I look at her picture but for a moment. The picture is special as it has both the power to sadden and reinvigorate me. I vividly re-call Tina's pain and horror, her screams of anguish. The picture evokes my feelings of hopelessness while I tried to comfort this innocent little angel when I arrived at the scene, and my sadness after the paramedics rushed her away. The picture also elicits the power I felt soon after the incident, the belief that there was something I could do. My spirit came alive and I said to myself, as if speaking directly to the perpetrator, "So, you want to terrorize the community and shoot little girls, do you? Well, I'm going to terrorize you. I have rules to follow but they won't stop me from relentlessly pursuing you and sending you to prison. Let the games begin!"

When I look at this picture in times of need, I stop worrying about all the insignificant little things I let get to me, about all the things that I possibly can't change right now. And, while I know that little Tina eventually recovered from her wounds and that the suspects were later identified and arrested, that picture is a powerful trigger that realigns my sense of purpose and re-fuels my passion for police work.

The trick of course, is to harness this power properly. When that picture delivers its shot of adrenaline, I don't dispense with my personal issues then run off breathing fire like a maniac. Rather, I focus my experience, knowledge and instincts to solve the problem at hand in the very best way that I can. It's always done ethically and professionally. It is done, and it is done well.

If you're on a gang unit and are going after someone who doesn't remember how many people he's shot this month and believes he probably won't live past thirty anyway, you must be mentally prepared, always. If your spirit is broken or if you are distracted by the minutiae of life, you'll be no match for a violent, dangerous criminal who places little value on a human life. An effective cop is one who can deal with their issues well, and can come back and gain that competitive spirit when required. After 28 years, I can still call tap that energy and use it to the advantage of my community and my fellow officers.

It is essential also to separate raw gang work from the other pressures of the job that you no doubt will face. I was once under investigation for excessive force stemming from an incident where two officers were attacked while patrolling a housing project. During the attack, numerous officers responded to the officers' request for assistance. As the situation ended and officers were leaving, someone threw a rock at a police car, and that started another brawl. Soon after the incident, my partner and I were accused of "thumping" a citizen and leaving the scene.

The thing was, we weren't even there! My partner and I were at a hospital with a rape victim. When Internal Affairs investigators began to interview me and treat me like I was guilty, I let them play their game. I knew where I was at the time and had numerous witnesses with great credibility, including doctors, nurses, and the victim, to vouch for me and my partner. We were wrongly accused and I believe we were treated poorly by investigators. When I walked out of that interview, I had to make a decision. Do I sulk and refuse to put any effort in my job because of the way I was treated by people on my own team, or do I go out and continue being an effective gang cop and show the Internal Affairs Division that they weren't going to get in the way of me taking care of business on the street? I suppose the I.A. folks believed they were just doing their job, but the experience didn't stop my partner and me from making a great arrest of a gang member for robbery right after that nasty interview. Making a good arrest has always made me feel like I'm of value to society, and validates my decision to be a gang cop. Helping someone in need or stopping trouble before it starts also provides the same satisfaction, a form of "spiritual" compensation that sustains me.

In your long and winding career, you will go through countless phases and changes. Accept those phases and changes and take care of yourself. Remember that it's a long road with enemies both inside and out. Continue on your journey and remember that managing these enemies well will keep you healthy, happy and productive.

3

Don't Get Bitter, Get Better

Adversity has the effect of eliciting talents, which in prosperous circumstances would have lain dormant.

HORACE

If your job takes you anywhere in or around the violent world of street gangs, rest assured that you will experience your fair share of adversity. If embraced and challenged, adversity will bring out the best in you and can help you grow and mature as a professional. But it can also consume and defeat you, if you allow the inherent frustrations to take hold of your psyche.

The ability to deal appropriately with adversity must be a career and personal imperative. While every human being in any field of endeavour ought to develop this skill, in law enforcement and in gang work, it can be a matter of life or death. In practical terms, you can't expect to safely or effectively deal with gang members on the street, in prison or in a courtroom when your spirit is broken or your mind is not totally in the moment, locked on the task at hand. After all, you may be dealing with a criminal who has the capacity to injure or kill someone in the morning, and then baptize their child in the afternoon. Gang members can be that unpredictable and insensitive.

My competitive spirit and drive to achieve have always allowed me to motivate myself when faced with adversity, both big and small. Years ago I learned from my parents, and later certain police officer peers, that despite the support structures that might be present around me (my family, my squad, the police brotherhood), that self-motivation was my responsibility. In other words, the will to improve and fight back must exist inside of you and remain accessible when you need it.

Especially in police, military and corrections settings, where work is guided within a hierarchical structure by rules, regulations, policies and procedures, one of the most ever-present water cooler topics of conversation is that of morale - or the lack of it. A police officer's morale can not only affected by these rules, but also by the quality of supervision received, court decisions, co-workers, working conditions and a host of other factors, including seemingly inconsequential things that might be said at roll-call or briefing. The link between morale and adversity is clear, and you need to deal with both properly.

The interesting thing about morale is that the raw gang work itself is normally not a contributing factor to one's decline in morale. Sure, you will experience adversity working gangs (arrests gone bad, devastating crime scenes, unjust court decisions), but being out on the street and involved in the "chase" can simultaneously free your mind from the challenges back at the station, yet focus it on the real - and mostly enjoyable - art of doing police work.

But this is not an automatic response; you must work hard at it. I always tried, before hitting the streets, to realistically assess and deal with my state of morale. It was just one of those pre-shift, checklist-type things I did, like inspecting my handgun or the power level of my police radio battery. I found that if I took the time to briefly reflect on the negative forces around me, that I could actually reconcile and set them aside in such a way as to not let them impact the level of my work performance. The fact that I made this morale-checking process a part of my routine, always made me more consistent in the field.

Now, I know what you are thinking: it's tough to stay positive when others around me are griping. Sure, negative and cynical attitudes can be contagious. My strategy is to simply try to avoid people like that or, if this can't be done, pay no attention to their bitching and moaning. As a supervisor who recruits and selects other officers to work within my unit, one of the first things I do is try to get a behind the scenes view of the candidate. Fundamentally, I try to determine whether the prospect in front of me is a positive or negative person. I can deal with an officer who needs to augment his skills through a more challenging assignment, but I can't deal with a person whose creed is "the cup is half empty". Trust me; I am not the only supervisor out there who considers negative people to be less desirable than positive people, even those who may have superior skills sets.

When it comes to setbacks in law enforcement, how you respond depends on the seriousness or degree of the setback. Many times that determines how fast you can bounce back, but it should not determine the intensity with which you come back.

Early in my career, I realized that working gangs was all that I really wanted to do. One of my earliest setbacks was not being selected to work on a CRASH (Community Resources Against Street Hoodlums) unit when I was a younger officer with about five years on the department. Before the Rampart scandal broke involving a couple of gang officers working in the Rampart Division, gang units on the LAPD were called CRASH units. Then, there weren't twenty-two gang units on the LAPD like there are today. In present day Los Angeles, all 18 geographic divisions or substations are divided into four bureaus, with each bureau and division having its own Special Enforcement Unit (SEU), which is responsible for policing gangs.

Back in the early '80s, there were only four bureau CRASH units, including one in the Central Bureau, which included my Newton Street Division. Central Bureau CRASH would usually recruit its officers from the divisions that were in Central Bureau because those officers usually knew their gangs. I felt that I knew the many violent gangs in Newton Street Division as well, if not better, than any of my counterparts. What made "Shootin' Newton" Division the unique station in Central Bureau was that it was the only one with a large concentration of Crips and Bloods gang members, which I had come to know well. The other divisions that comprised the Central Bureau, namely Rampart, Hollenbeck, Northeast and Central were, and still are, dominated by Hispanic gang activity.

I had many friends in Central Bureau CRASH at that time. Many of them were recruited into the unit from divisions other than Newton Street so, consequently, some were not that comfortable around Crips and Bloods. Since many of the officers were reluctant to deal with these gangs - and since I knew so much about them and had signalled my desire to work within this unit - I figured I would be a really good fit. The more I thought about it, the more I wanted to get in that CRASH unit, and was very pleased when I was loaned to the unit for one month, something that normally happens right before you are transferred there.

During my month-long stint, I was assigned to an officer who had been there awhile and was one of the more vocal, and perhaps most controversial, in the unit. We got off to a rocky start because he assumed I was another eager young guy who would do anything to get in the unit, including kiss his butt. He was also of the attitude that he was going to teach me gangs the right way; his way.

The first couple of days of my assignment saw us in Hollenbeck Division on routine patrols. On the third day, however, my temporary partner and I traveled into Newton Street Division, my home turf. About 8:00 pm, the following radio call was broadcast: "All Newton units in the vicinity ... 415 woman with a gun at 47th Street and Broadway. The woman is wearing a yellow dress and has the gun in her dress pocket. Code 2".

We were a block away when the call came out, so we were the first officers at the scene. The woman in the yellow dress was standing on the corner waving her arms at us. I recognized her immediately from prior contacts that we'd had. She was a 60-year old black woman who lived alone and bore the brunt of local gangsters who would get their kicks by throwing rocks at her house. I even knew her name and precisely where she lived.

As we exited our police car, my partner immediately drew down on her with his gun. I yelled, advising him that I knew her - I even called her by name in an attempt to reduce the temperature of the incident. Instantly, I could tell from her body language that she recognized me. I told her to keep her hands up, which she did as I approached her. Despite her obvious compliance, my partner still wanted to forcefully lay her down face-first on the street. Once I reached her - arms still in the air - I pulled out a black cap pistol from her dress pocket. Since she had no other weapons, we notified the dispatcher that there was a "Code 4" at the location. Everything was OK.

She then proceeded to tell us that the gangsters were throwing rocks at her house again, and the only thing she could think of doing to stop them was to try to scare them off with a cap pistol. Needless to say, this was not a particularly smart thing for her to do, but in her mind, she felt she had no other option. I scolded her for endangering herself, and suggested that we would give her extra patrol and try to catch whoever was throwing the rocks.

As we left the scene, I thought to myself that I had done a pretty good job of taking care of a potentially dangerous situation. I brought to bear my knowledge of the community with a dignified and patient approach, and believed that the incident would help solidify my spot on the CRASH unit. I felt relieved, and shuddered at the thought of the public's response, had my partner actually shot the frustrated black lady who was just trying to protect herself and her home from gangbangers with a harmless cap pistol.

My sense of relief was short-lived, however, as barely a minute later my partner pulled the car over and lambasted me, screaming, "That's the stupidest thing that I've ever seen anyone do!"

I said, "Well, proning out an old black woman who is being terrorized by a bunch of punks would be pretty close." I went on, "I knew that lady. Didn't you hear me call her by her name? Did she appear hostile toward us? Did she make any furtive movements? It seems to me that you don't know much about people and you don't have the instinct for this job. Now we probably have to go to the station because that poor old black lady made you mess your pants."

"You don't want to work our unit, do you?" he retorted. "I'll make it so a guy like you never gets in the unit. I thought that they said you were a good cop!"

"You can just take me to the station," I replied calmly. "If your idea of doing gang work is giving out chicken-shit tickets and shooting old ladies, I'll go back to Newton Division."

I imagine that there have been officers who wanted to get into that unit very bad and who actually took the abuse to get in, but I wasn't so inclined. I finished out my month-long loan, mostly working with him with not much happening. I got along with everyone else on the unit except this guy, the one who was going to evaluate me.

A few months had passed and other officers from Newton Street had been transferred to Central Bureau CRASH. Some of those officers didn't even have an interest in working gangs, but they wanted to escape patrol and its incessant radio calls. I was being passed over time and time again.

I finally confronted the lieutenant in charge of the unit. Although he didn't really know me, he told me that my reputation was that of an out of control officer. I thought, "Out of control? What the hell does that mean?" I left the meeting broken hearted. I couldn't work gangs. When I thought about it, I knew my "evaluator" had back-stabbed me. Unfortunately, no one else in that unit (including my friends) was going to stick their neck out for me and endorse me. I respected their decision because those guys had to work there and their lieutenant had a reputation for being vindictive about "defiant" officers.

I had come to a very important cross-road in my career. I asked myself whether I should accept this set-back and continue to work patrol, waiting for another speciality assignment. Or do I fight back, and double my efforts to win a job working gangs?

I decided to turn my situation around, and use the rejection as a motivator to become the best damned gang cop on the Los Angeles Police Department, whether I was on a CRASH unit or not. I was going to show them that they had made a mistake.

I became more dedicated to my work because I was on a well-defined and compelling mission. Every time the Central Bureau CRASH was in Newton Division looking for a wanted suspect, I made it my priority to get him first, so that I could walk into their office with my catch and say, "You looking for this guy?"

My detractors eventually got sick of me, as I outperformed them. I didn't let them beat me. I was bringing in suspects that they couldn't find. I was also helping them solve crimes with the informants whom I had carefully cultivated.

In retrospect, I'm glad I was turned away initially, as it made me want a CRASH unit posting even more. The feeling of being on the outside looking into a place I knew I deserved to be was indeed disappointing, but it also propelled me to be the best that I could be. I could have gotten bitter, but instead I got better.

My experience, though, is insignificant compared to the many stories of ordinary people who, in the face of great adversity, have marshalled the passion to change the world. Learning from their experiences will give you some real perspective, and prove the point that adversity can build, rather than destroy.

Consider the story of a man who is well known within law enforcement circles: John Walsh, host of *America's Most Wanted: America Fights Back* and leading international advocate for victim's rights.

John Walsh never set out to be a world famous crime fighter and fugitive hunter. In the summer of 1981, Walsh was a partner in a hotel management company in Hollywood, Florida. He and his wife, Reve, had a six-year-old son, Adam, and never thought crime could touch them. But their lives were changed forever on July 27th, 1981, when Adam was abducted and later found murdered.

It wasn't long after Adam's death that the Walshes turned their grief into positive energy to help missing and exploited children. Battling bureaucratic resistance and legislative nightmares, John and Reve's work led to the passage of the Missing Children Act of 1982 and the Missing Children's Assistance Act of 1984. The latter Bill founded the National Center for Missing and Exploited Children, which maintains a toll-free hotline number (1-800-THE-LOST) to report a missing child or the sighting of one.

Today, Walsh continues his lobbying efforts, testifying before Congress and state legislatures on crime, missing children and victims' issues.

John Walsh and his wife experienced a devastating incident that could have crippled them forever. But the Walshes used this experience to change the world. They could have gotten bitter, but instead, they got better.

4

Knowledge is a Mountain to Climb

Every day you may make progress. Every step may be fruitful. Yet there will stretch out before you an ever-lengthening, ever-ascending, ever-improving path. You know you will never get to the end of the journey. But this, so far from discouraging, only adds to the joy and glory of the climb.

SIR WINSTON CHURCHILL

Most successful and dedicated police officers get so involved in their work that they seldom stop to take inventory of what they know. When they do, however, they are often surprised to discover the sheer amount of knowledge they have gained. In my experience, this can be both personally satisfying as well as slightly disheartening, as it can remind us that we have been walking around underestimating ourselves all along.

That's why it is important, as you continue on in your career, to periodically look down and see how far you've climbed up the mountain of knowledge. Stop your climb, take in the view for a moment, correct your course if necessary, and continue your climb. The trick is, of course, to avoid the hidden crevices and to not stop your climb for too long, because you will eventually get passed by others who are striving for the summit.

Law enforcement is very competitive. You have already beaten the odds by actually being in law enforcement, since the majority of people who attempt to have a career in our field are screened out for one reason or another. But once you are there, the real competition starts. Everything is based upon measuring up to your peers. I know that in our department, everything from promotions to assignments are based on you versus the person next to you. Sometimes these decisions are made based not on your actual value and track record, but upon others' perception of how you measure up compared to your peers. Whatever the basis of decision, your existing knowledge – and your willingness to keep forging ahead – will keep you ahead of the game, but still can be loaded with pitfalls. Let me explain.

As I describe in Chapter 3, I initially couldn't get into the CRASH gang unit because I was perceived by the lieutenant in charge as "out of control". In retrospect, I believe that his perception of me was based on my high level of activity and knowledge regarding gangs in my jurisdiction. For some, these traits would be judged as desirable, but for others (perhaps those not confident in their own ability to manage or in their own knowledge) these traits could be intimidating or perceived negatively. I recall an old military saying that is appropriate here: if you get too far out in front of your fellow troops, you'll begin to look like the enemy. Perhaps the lieutenant thought I couldn't follow his direction or that he couldn't control me. Whatever the reason, it was clear to me that my knowledge, in part, actually hurt me.

Does that mean you should fly below the radar, learning only as much as you need to stay slightly ahead of your peers, but not so much as to distance yourself from them? Is too much knowledge a bad thing? Of course not, but you do need to understand that superior knowledge is no guarantee of success.

Despite the set-back noted above, I continued to climb my mountain, secure in the knowledge that in the long run it would propel me forward within my police agency. That's the thing about knowledge - sometimes there are immediate pay-offs to your investment of time and energy, but generally, it can take a while for your efforts to produce rewards. You must be patient, at times seeking opportunities to display your knowledge; at other times trusting that informed, honest and confident superiors will see and exploit the value of your expertise.

In my case, the CRASH rejection forced me to re-double my efforts to learn the gangs in my area. Even though I had reached the point where I felt I was the predominant expert on a particular gang, I continued to climb. Even after a newspaper article about me appeared, highlighting that I was the original "Pacman" (the same Pacman whose nickname and yellow Plymouth Fury police vehicle were used in the 1988 movie *Colors* starring Robert Duvall and Sean Penn), I continued to climb, choosing not to rest on my laurels. That would have been good enough for some people, but it wasn't for me. Seventeen years later, I am still climbing, and sincerely feel that I passed many experts going up the mountain because I was able to stay motivated and sincere about the work. While my investment in learning has not always paid off, on balance, it has served me well and brought me closer to my summit.

Aside from the possibility of resentment, your knowledge may also motivate others to try to minimize it or attempt to take it away from you. I was once cross-examined in a gang-related court proceeding and was asked by a defense attorney, "Isn't it true that the actual experts on gangs on the Los Angeles Police Department are the officers assigned to CRASH?". I replied, "No, that isn't necessarily true. CRASH is an assignment. Expertise is a very personal thing. I am the Department's expert on this particular gang. I have contact with the members on a daily basis and know them as well as any other officer on our department."

The knowledge you gain in the course of your life and in the course of your work are yours and yours alone. You're the one who earned what you know, and no one should be allowed to take that knowledge away from you. Some people may disagree with you, and others may fail to act upon or even misuse your knowledge and guidance. Some people will even take credit for your knowledge (I know, real hard to believe). But when you've done your job right and have learned it well, your knowledge cannot be co-opted – unless, of course, you allow it to be.

Back in the early 1980s, rock cocaine hit the streets of South-Central Los Angeles and turned the world of Crips and

Bloods topsy-turvy. For the first time, many of the gangsters began to have money, and I mean real money. With money came cars, clothes, guns, jewellery and anything else it could buy. These guys in South-Central also had connections and influence, since they got in on the ground floor of dealing rock cocaine throughout the United States, not just Los Angeles.

As the money began to flow in earnest, gang dynamics changed and two main competing groups coalesced, comprised mostly of gangsters from a variety of gangs. The battle lines drawn, the two groups engaged in a fierce war with each other over control of the trade of rock cocaine. So, not only did we have traditional gang wars in L.A., we had self-styled organized crime groups at war with each other over the sale of a substance that could deliver real wealth.

At that time, I had the opportunity to work with a couple of great officers assigned to Newton Street Division. Given the size of the problem, we worked together to document all the players, rock houses, drug connections and crimes associated with these two groups. Through some diligent investigative work and a lot of shoe leather, we were also able to determine that these two groups were involved in at least twenty-five homicides in Los Angeles in the preceding months. We did the research on our own because we sensed a major problem with the formation of these groups and others like them. We weren't directed to assess this particular problem. We just didn't wait to be asked to learn what we figured we needed to know, for everyone's sake.

When we felt the time was right and that we could support our theory regarding these groups with documentation (including link charts of all of our information), we presented our findings to our superiors. Now, you have to remember, we were at the lowly rank of police officer. The stuff we were getting involved with was normally handled by Narcotics Division or Organized Crime Division. We were the bottom of the food chain and we were on to something that the "experts" didn't know was going on. We knew we were going to be scrutinized, to put it politely.

A meeting was held with selected members of the command staff of the Department. They were all the heads of any Departmental entity that could be affected by this information. Naturally, the meeting was of a sensitive nature. We made a presentation to the contingent, making sure to be in-depth regarding our documentation. There were a couple of captains who didn't want to buy in on this. It must have been disturbing to them because the information was coming from mere police officers and not their experienced investigators. We received great support from some homicide detectives who attended the meeting and were able to connect their homicides to our subjects. We concluded the meeting and everyone was ordered not to discuss any of the information to any outsiders. It was top secret until the Department decided what the next step would be.

Well, someone in the meeting decided to take action for the whole group anyway. The information was leaked to the L.A. Times and appeared in the next day's paper. The drug dealers who had no idea we were onto them, now knew, greatly compromising our ability to make arrests. My two partners and I screamed bloody murder and asked that the leak be investigated. Regrettably, we never discovered who the mole was.

Despite the leak and the damage caused as a result, to combat these emergent drug gangs the Department decided to combine all the "big boys", including members of our Narcotics Division - Major Violators Squad and personnel from our Organized Crime and Intelligence Division (OCID). I knew from experience that none of these guys really wanted to follow crazy-ass gangsters with machine guns and money in South-Central L.A. The narcotics guys would rather be chasing down Colombians and the OCID guys would rather be watching old thugs in leisure suits having martinis on Ventura Boulevard. This combined squad was to follow some of the main leaders of these groups and try to make a dope case, since drugs seemed to be the tie-in with all of their activities.

Because of our previous research, we were ordered to attend the first briefing of this new task force. We were to brief them on the information that we had gathered and then keep our noses out of it because we were getting in "over our heads".

What happened at that first briefing was a prime example of others trying to take my knowledge away from me. My partners and I walked in and were asked to present our findings to thirty pissed off major leaguers. No one was the least bit cordial to us, particularly since they were ordered against their will to listen to what we "wannabes" had to say. We detailed the beginning of our investigation and led them right up to the present day activities we carefully uncovered. We also profiled the main leaders within the drug groups, and detailed their likely whereabouts, activities and associates. While many questions were directed our way from the sceptics, we were able to handle each and every one of them.

Then it got ugly. Some irate veteran asked in a pointed fashion, "How do we know this is true?" This guy must have been one of the kings of the jungle, because no one took exception to the discourteous tone of his voice.

"It's true because we just told you it was true," I said. "We've supported the information with documentation and with corroboration from various independent sources".

Then Mr. King of the Jungle asked my partner equally aggressively, "Well then who's your snitch?", as if to say that we were somehow incapable of doing top-quality police work.

My partner replied, "I don't have a snitch." Good answer.

He looked at me and said, "Who is your snitch?" A room full of sharks were just waiting for the answer from the punk police officer.

We had been disrespected enough, so I decided to give them a taste of their own medicine by responding. "I don't have a snitch".

"What do you mean you don't have a snitch?" he snarled.

"Yes. I got the information from an anonymous caller. I don't know why he picked me, but he's always right on the money with his info." The lion's big, red nose got bigger and redder. He knew that I was lying, I knew that I was lying, everyone knew I was lying. I also knew that according to LAPD policy, they couldn't take me outside and pull my toenails out.

We stuck by our information. This squad later went out and couldn't find any of the targets. After two days, they called us and we located the targets for them. They followed the targets for a couple of days and reported back that there was no activity. We kind of figured that they were going to do that because they didn't want this assignment to begin with.

The rest is history. All of the drug trafficking, murders, drug rip-offs, corruption, gang migration, money laundering, new cars, money, weapons ... all of it, are well documented in the world of gangs and drugs. The 1980s were the "Crazy 80s" in the gang world of Los Angeles. The gangs of LA and their influence made quite an impact throughout the country and even in other parts the world.

Ultimately, the two main drug trafficking groups finally disbanded due to police pressure (from street coppers), jail, treachery, death and taxes. Our information was good. We stuck by it despite the fact others didn't want to believe it or hear of it. The main weapon we defended ourselves with in that room full of hostile experts was our knowledge. We trusted it and were committed to it, and it served us well. Stay committed to your mission, to your climb, to your mountain. Your knowledge is your mountain ... the fall will be your fall.

5

Cultivate and Project a Four Aces Mentality

Self-confidence is the first requisite to great undertakings.

SAMUEL JOHNSON

If you are playing poker and happen to hold four aces, my bet says you're going to win the hand. It doesn't matter how much bluffing is going on around you - you've got a hand that is virtually unbeatable

Now, I know what you experienced poker-playing folks out there are thinking: "Moreno doesn't play much poker. If he did, he'd know that a royal flush beats four aces every time!" Well, besides not making for a particularly pleasant-sounding chapter title (can you imagine the imagery associated with "Cultivate and project a royal flush mentality"!!), my choice in selecting the four aces metaphor is a deliberate one.

Let's turn to the world of sports for some convenient illustrations. In his peak with the Chicago Bulls, Michael Jordan was the best in the business and was on any given night virtually unstoppable. You knew - and he knew - that he was probably going to net 35 points and gain ten-plus assists. So dominating was his presence that many opponents' games would falter, as if they were content to watch the master in action from the very best front row seats in the house. Wayne Gretzky had the same effect in his days with the Edmonton Oilers, and so too did Joe Montana when he took charge of the huddle with his San Francisco 49'ers teammates. Today, Tiger Woods perhaps best illustrates an athlete who is at the top of his game, and brings a four aces mentality to his work, particularly when he is playing in one of the four PGA "major" tournaments.

While I don't know these athletes personally, I am willing to bet the family ranch that they were well aware of their talent and had believed in their ability to win despite the challenges that they faced. However, I don't think they believed that every victory was certain. Like most peak performers I know, my sense is that they were aware that on any given day, an opponent could rise to the occasion and produce defeat – someone could, despite the odds, produce a royal flush to beat their four aces. This prospect of defeat, I believe, is what made them practice, train, prepare and remain disciplined in their approach to be the best they could possibly be.

As a police officer, your goal should be to ensure that your expertise gives you the very same feeling and produces the very same result. It should not matter what's going on around you or who is doing what. You know what you know, and you know it well, period. This applies to you when you are out in the field on patrol or conducting an investigation, or when you participate in a court case.

It's a natural thing to doubt yourself at times, especially if you're about to testify as an expert in a trial. That's because you care about your knowledge and reputation. Fortunately, a little self-doubt keeps you honest and makes you invest the time and effort to prepare.

Along with the growth of the gang problem in North America has come a similar expansion in the number and variety of real and self-appointed gang experts testifying for the defense. It used to be that the only person in the courtroom who might know more about gangs than you was the defendant. However, the size of today's gang "industry", if we can call it that, means that there is money to be made by academic experts, community activists, retired police officers, former corrections officials and others, who are more than willing to challenge your expertise on behalf of the accused in a Court of Law. While some of these so-called experts don't deserve their title, many are very talented and have, if the circumstances are right and the stars align, the ability to beat you one-on-one. Today, more than ever before, you need to go the extra mile to prepare yourself if you are qualified by a Judge to act as an expert witness for the prosecution.

Before you seek or accept this most important assignment and esteemed designation, you need to ensure that you are, in fact, an expert, which comes from all the things that make up your personal knowledge. What does this mean as far as gangs are concerned? If you're asked to testify about a gang, take the time to know, among other things, its history, culture, folklore, boundaries, symbols, number of members (inside and outside of prison), tattoos, criminal activities, entry/exit rites, affiliations, enemies, modes of communication, dress codes, hang-outs, attitudes when dealing with law enforcement, leadership, support structures and links to legitimate business.

If you're going to testify on an individual gang member, you need to be able to articulate, in a clear, concise and compelling manner, why the subject is a gang member. Some of the more obvious factors in determining gang membership are self-admittance, tattoos, hand signs, clothing, photographs with other gang members and documentation that connects the subject with gang activity. When testifying, think lowest common denominator. That is, present your facts as if you are talking to a juror that has no prior knowledge of or background in gangs. Start with the most obvious factors and work your way through the facts in a logical and thorough manner. Be objective and don't become personally involved in making the guy a gang member. All you can say is what you know.

Back in the mid 1980s, I was contacted by an FBI agent out of Tacoma, Washington who wanted to interview me regarding some L.A. gang members who were arrested for dealing cocaine. They met with me and asked if I could identify some gang members from a series of photographs. It just so happened that I knew this particular gang very well, so I was able to identify every person, by proper name and moniker. The agents were elated with this new cache of information, and I later received a subpoena for the case that was being held in federal court in Tacoma.

Part of the defense team's strategy in defending these gang members was to suggest that although they were from L.A., they didn't know each other and were all in Tacoma by sheer coincidence. Clearly, my testimony was essential to show that they were all from the same gang, which in turn, would help prove the existence of a conspiracy.

The U.S. Attorney handling the case hid me in the court hallway because he didn't want them to know that I was going to testify. For two days, I could hear the gang members being brought into court shackled together for safety purposes. From my concealed vantage point, they seemed quite arrogant and belligerent, and my sense was that they tried to intimidate key individuals involved with the case, a commonplace strategy amongst gang members.

When the day came for me to testify, I proudly entered the courtroom, confident in the knowledge that I had the stuff necessary to help convict those who were accused of drug trafficking. Much like Ebenezer Scrooge in *The Christmas Carol*, these gang members looked like they had just seen a ghost. Despite the previous arrogance and bravado, theirs was a look of a poker player sitting across the table from an opponent who just unveiled four aces.

I walked in, nodded at all of them, and proceeded to the witness stand. The U.S. Attorney who was questioning me asked me to state my experience, background and expertise, which the court accepted. I was then asked if I knew the defendants who were seated with their attorneys at the defense side of the room. I say the defense side of the room because there were too many accused - eight in total - to have just a single defense table! One by one, I named each defendant by real name, moniker, gang affiliation and length of time I had personally known each of them. My knowledge nailed them. It was one of the easiest testimonies I'd ever given because I knew them so well. Perhaps an indication of the strength of my testimony, I only received one question on cross-examination dealing with a matter incidental to the crime but relating to a possible sentence reduction for one gang member who assisted me in a previous rape case.

All of the accused were convicted, and the kicker was that I really didn't do anything. All the hard digging was done by the F.B.I., the Tacoma Police Department and the U.S. Attorney's Office. The gangsters assumed that I was the mastermind of the whole operation. I just happened to know what the authorities needed to know to lock down their case. The good news for you is that the prerequisite for cultivating and projecting a four aces mentality is not necessarily many years of police service. We probably all know someone with twenty years of experience in their chosen field, but which essentially consists of one year of experience twenty times over. And yet, we all know that there are relative newbies in the profession, who produce big results.

Starting as an eighteen year old, in the seven-year period from 1979 to 1986, his first seven in the National Hockey League, Wayne Gretzky generated 1337 points, almost one-half of his lifetime production in the first one-third of his career. In my 28 years of service, I have met several young officers who display the same level of productivity – individuals who took their job seriously, invested considerable energy to learn their trade and the environment around them, and then put up big numbers in the field and in court.

It's not about sheer talent, although that helps. It's really about desire, passion, discipline and commitment, knowing full well that even if you exercise and exert these traits, someone still could unveil a royal flush in court. It's this that keeps you on the edge, pushing the envelope to be the very best you can possibly be.

6

Know the Ocean That Surrounds Your Island

Someone's sitting in the shade today because someone planted a tree a long time ago.

WARREN BUFFETT

If you want to be effective at working gangs, you must be open minded, creative, and willing to dig up and assimilate knowledge.

Early in my career when I was working patrol, I had a deep interest in gangs, especially the Crip and Blood gangs. In between radio calls, I would spend my available time learning about and interacting with Crip and Blood gang members. Before I knew it, I had a great deal of knowledge about these gangs and their leaders in my division.

One of the first things I learned is that while gang members claim turf and neighborhoods, they don't respect boundaries. In their world, they don't have to. To them, the enemy is the enemy, regardless of whether the enemy neighborhood is in an adjacent city, police division or county. If they want to attack, they bring their fight to the enemy.

Years ago, a Blood gang in the south end of our division was getting decimated by a Crip gang from an unincorporated region of Los Angeles County that we bordered. While the Crip gang neighborhood was essentially on the other side of a major street, it happened to be in the County and therefore out of our patrol region. In a very real sense, within yards of each other, two

51

worlds resided since separate law enforcement agencies handled the two competing gangs.

Since "our gang" was being victimized by "their gang", I decided to take a drive to the neighboring law enforcement agency and get their take on the war between the gangs. Little did I know that my visit to the Firestone Substation of Los Angles County Sheriffs Department (LASD) would make me awestruck.

Their gang deputies were assigned to a unit called "OSS" which stood for Operation Safe Streets, the designation for their station's gang units. I introduced myself and made it clear that I was there to get information and learn, not to take something from them, never to be seen again. I explained that we had a real problem with one of their gangs and I was there to learn what I could about the gang and it's most influential members. The OSS deputies were busy, but they took the time to "school me" on their gang and its members.

I was amazed by how much these deputies knew about their gangs. I certainly had a good handle on my gangs, but these guys were at a completely different level as far as gang knowledge was concerned. So impressive was their gang expertise that I resolved to become a real gang expert and therefore reach and operate at the same level.

I was also shocked to learn that they had informants within our gangs, but never had ongoing or consistent contact with the LAPD's CRASH units. The LASD deputies would contact an LAPD homicide unit or CRASH unit when they had information that might help solve a crime, but for the most part, there was no collaboration because of the geographical boundaries.

Through these informants, the LASD deputies had collected valuable intelligence about our gangs. I learned first hand from these experienced deputies the extent to which gang members gather intelligence about their enemies. I learned that when a gang member decides he's going to "talk" to the police, he's more likely to snitch off an enemy than his own homeboy. Sometimes he has no choice in the matter, but all other things being equal, he'd rather snitch on the enemy.

The LASD deputies reinforced the rationale of encouraging a gang member to talk to me. For the gang member, he thinks it keeps him on your good side as you perceive him as being cooperative and friendly towards you. As well, it allows you to take care of his business against the enemy. It minimizes the risk to him and his fellow gangsters from that enemy. He can sit back and watch you seek out and arrest his enemy for some murder or robbery. He keeps his hands clean and doesn't have to get involved in any criminal activity against his enemy. He stays alive and out of jail or prison. The enemy is removed.

The Firestone OSS deputies had their gangsters talking to them about our gangs. Nobody on our end seemed interested in the information. Luckily for me, these deputies were open to developing an ongoing, working relationship. Up until that time, the professional jealousy between the Los Angeles Sheriff's Department and the Los Angeles Police Department prevented a lot of work from getting done. Sure, there were exceptions, but for the most part we lived in our world and they lived in theirs. It took awhile to figure out that our worlds sometimes collide.

That eye opening experience made me realize that the location of the Firestone LASD substation was adjacent to only one of the borders of my Newton Street Division. I wondered what was going on all around my division. I quickly made contact with patrol and gang officers in Southwest Division on our western border, 77th Division on our southwestern border, Hollenbeck Division to our east and Central Division to the north. I also made a contact in Rampart Division because one of our gangs had a large clique in that division. Beside the valuable gang information links I was developing for myself, I was able to get a more accurate picture of the gang problem in my division. It made me better at responding to gang activity and anticipating potential problems such as retaliation and emerging feuds. My work would also make the officers in the surrounding divisions and jurisdictions better at what they did, as I reciprocated information freely.

Years of gang experience tell me that if you walk into a gang information-sharing meeting and there are 75 law enforcement professionals in attendance, there will be at least five people who you really should get to know. They will be the people whose area borders on your area, whose caseload contains members of your gang or whose jail or prison incarcerates your gang members. Those are the people you need to know, and they need to know you.

Now, when I travel around North America conducting training on gangs, I observe many different attitudes and methods amongst law enforcement officers in respect to dealing with gangs. I once conducted a gang training session for some parents in the city of Ottawa, Ontario, Canada. In attendance were some officers from the Gatineau Police Service in Quebec, a bordering Canadian province. These officers had the mindset that there might be something at our training session that would help them. On a regular basis, kids and teenagers cross the bridge from the City of Ottawa and venture into Gatineau to enjoy the city's vibrant nightlife. Despite the real boundaries that separate the two cities (e.g., a major river and two different political jurisdictions), those officers were open to receiving new information and to cultivating professional relationships. That is an example of being progressive and proactive in looking at your gang problem. That is an example of officers wanting to know more.

I have also seen 77th Division officers working with Southeast Division officers, New Jersey State Police officers working with NYPD officers, "feds" working with "locals", and I could go on and on. The point is that we sometimes set our own boundaries.

I praise organizations like the California Gang Investigators Association (CGIA), the California Gang Task Force (CGTF), the East Coast Gang Investigators Association (ECGIA) and the many other organizations forming throughout the law enforcement world. These organizations promote excellence in gang work by providing training and the opportunity to network with other professionals facing the same challenges.

So the lesson in this chapter is simple. The neighborhood or gang that you focus your energy on is like your island. It's not enough to know what's happening on your island. Take the time to know the ocean that surrounds your island.

7

What Motivates Others Should Be Important To You

Ability is what you're capable of doing. Motivation determines what you do. Attitude determines how well you do it.

LOU HOLTZ

People are motivated by different things. For your well-being, you need to know what motivates the people you deal with, including your peers, supervisors, subordinates, and even gang members themselves. Understanding the source, form and content of other's motivation outside of your work is also essential. Why is that person complimenting me? Why does that young man want to marry my daughter? Why does my spouse seem to avoid dealing with serious family matters? Why does my son want to get into law enforcement? The answers to these kinds of questions are critical, as this can help determine the manner in which you deal with these individuals.

In working gangs, understanding what motivates the people you deal with - especially gang members - is even more important, and can even be a matter of life or death.

As I have stressed elsewhere in this book, it is essential to learn how to talk and develop a rapport with gang members. I believe that one of the characteristics that differentiates a great gang cop from just an average one is his or her skills and effectiveness in pulling useful and viable information from a gang member. Just as it is important to understand what a gang member is saying to you, it is essential to understand why the gangster is talking to you. In effect, you are obtaining information from someone who would prefer not to give it up, so what is he thinking? What does he believe is in it for him?

Gang members will talk to you for a variety of reasons, and I generally classify their motivations in two categories: going away from motivations (they want to avoid something), and going towards motivations (they want something from you). For instance, they will talk to you in order to stay on your good side so that you will give them a break or not mess with them. They will talk to you in order to keep you on what I like to call "consignment". In other words, they'll tell you things so that if and when they get in trouble or arrested, they can call on you from lock-up with a request that goes something like this: "Remember when I gave you that info?....now I need some help from you."

They'll also talk to you to obtain money. In my entire career, I think I've actually paid informants only four or five times, and only did so because the informants actually needed the money to get by. Usually when a gang member gives you information for money, the quality of the information isn't as good as the information coming from a person who needs a favor or wants to stay on your good side. Whenever possible, try to avoid informants who are principally motivated by money.

Gang members will talk to you in order to get even with someone, or simply to eliminate their enemy by helping put them in jail. This is okay by me because I will do the same thing against them if their enemy snitches them off. Call it one of the laws of the gang jungle.

Potential victims are good sources of information, too. Some of the best information I have ever received has come from people who thought that they were going to be killed by a particular gang member. They usually owe someone money or have ripped somebody off. They want to snitch off their potential killer in order to save their own ass. This type of information, like snitching off an enemy, is usually good.

Gang members of the opposite sex will also tell you things to see if they can start up a personal relationship with you. Once you get personally involved with an informant, especially of the opposite sex, you are compromised. End of story. They can then manipulate you. They can use you to gain information about your unit, agency or investigation. Remember, if it seems too good to be true, it probably is.

It is also important to know what motivates the people with whom you work alongside; those who are supposedly on the same side as you. If you are a dedicated professional attempting to become more effective in your profession, you'll need to deal with effective people. The effective people are usually the ones who are the most dedicated. Sounds simple, but it's not that easy to figure out those who are really dedicated from those who simply pretend to be.

I have been around officers who try to take shortcuts to their knowledge and expertise. Can't be done. You can take short cuts to your reputation, but that will eventually catch up to you. Your reputation must be earned one inch at a time, one street corner at a time, one interview at a time, one arrest at a time.

People who are dedicated in their craft are open-minded and willing to learn. People who are selfish in their ways are controlled by their ego. They are motivated by their need to be above everyone else, whether it is in knowledge, acclaim or reputation. Their mission in life is to stay above the rest, as if on a pedestal. They are the ones who won't help other officers improve. Anybody with knowledge is perceived as a threat to them - the more knowledge, the greater the threat. Remember the officer from the east coast in Chapter 1 who suggested that their "local" expert didn't want outsiders coming in to provide training, even though they desperately needed it? Any outsider was a threat to his kingdom. That so-called expert wasn't working to get better or improve those around him. He was working to maintain and protect his reputation and standing.

Since I travel frequently throughout North America on speaking engagements, I am exposed to a tremendous diversity of law enforcement talent and have, as a result, finely honed my sense of perception of people. I always find it interesting how people respond to me as a respected expert, as that tells me much about who they are and what drives them. I've worked gangs for a long time and I'm good at it. I earned and enjoy the Pacman reputation, and I belong to one of the premiere law enforcement agencies in the world which, for better or for worse, is at the fore-front in the war against gangs.

When I speak at a seminar, the sincere and dedicated people are the ones who talk to me and are willing to learn. Not only are they willing to learn, they are willing to share. By sharing, they are teaching, and therefore I learn all the time.

The threatened ones are easy to pick out of a crowd. They are cold and distant, like the poker player who keeps his cards very close to his vest and never cracks a smile. They normally are too busy and don't have the time for a beer and a good talk with the troops. They don't want to compare notes, expose their own knowledge or share stories from the field. They're the ones who say "it doesn't work that way around here", as if to say that either the gang phenomenon or the strategies to deal with it are some-how different where they're from. The unfortunate thing is that people like this are missing a great opportunity to expand their universe, and to get to know other professionals who share their same mission and may indeed have knowledge that can make them even better - or safer. If you are threatened by the knowl-edge of those with whom you work, then you'd better examine your own motivations. The only one who should be a threat to your knowledge is a defense attorney or his gang expert.

Professionals who are motivated to be the best they can be in the war on gangs are the type of people you want to deal with. Experts who are consumed with making a name for themselves at the expense of others are people you want to avoid. Once you know what makes a person tick, you can better judge their sin-cerity. The more sincere they are, the more value they have to you.

There are well-meaning and dedicated people everywhere in the law enforcement community. You just need to find them. In a typical gang meeting, there may be 50 to 100 professionals in attendance. You may be familiar with 20 or 30 people, but only 5 to 10 will be of real value to you. Find them and get to know them. If you come across as being sincere, unselfish and trustworthy you will attract others who share your values. When you do things for others, they will normally reciprocate. When they can trust you, they will work for you . . . gang member or fellow cop.

Over the years, I've had my share of enemies and detractors on my side of the badge. When I reflect on these people over my career, most of them have one thing in common: they didn't like the way I worked. They felt that my work made them look bad or inferior. The truth is that my work had nothing to do with them. I wasn't stealing information or taking something that belonged to them. It was just that they didn't want to see me succeed because it reflected poorly upon them. In a sense, this attitude is the competitive spirit in law enforcement in its mutant form. I was working at my level for my own interests, but paradoxically it offended others.

Early in my career, it would hurt my feelings to think that a few fellow officers didn't like me. I wanted everyone to like me and it would really bother me if they did not. When I figured out why they didn't like me, I realized that it was their problem. They didn't like me for their own selfish reasons. When I understood their motivation, it was simple to deal with. I wasn't going to revert to their level of work for their sake. I was going to be me, because in reality, I wasn't doing anything wrong.

The cycle has remained the same over the years. I will get criticized or badmouthed by someone who is caught up in their own importance. That will motivate me to shut them up. Good work, good consistent police work, shuts them up every time. If you want to prove somebody wrong, do good work. They will eventually go away and find another enemy. Ultimately, it comes down to understanding the motivations of others; know them, and you'll soon be able to tell apart those who will help you from those who will hurt you.

8

Only When You Are in Control Are You Safe

Whatever you do, you need courage. Whatever course you decide upon, there is always someone to tell you that you are wrong. There are always difficulties arising that tempt you to believe your critics are right. To map out a course of action and follow it to an end requires some of the same courage that a soldier needs. Peace has its victories, but it takes brave men and women to win them.

RALPH WALDO EMERSON

As I indicated earlier, as a probationary officer I had the good fortune of being teamed up with an experienced officer who took the time to share his vast knowledge and equip me with bedrock skills to be safe and effective.

This individual was unique, and he definitely was misunderstood. Fitting in with the other officers with whom he worked wasn't a priority or even anything he really thought about. He was secure in his own skin and didn't try to impress others with fancy possessions, or ingratiate himself to others by hanging out with the crowd making small talk. He had a good handle of who he was as a person and a street cop, and prided himself on his excellent knowledge, level of activity, morality and work ethic. Perhaps what I liked most about him was his courage and passion for police work, and his ability to be a peak performer without needing anyone's blessing or pat on the back.

In the dark and violent world of the street cop, we often go home and tell our spouse, family and friends that we are the front line warrior who sticks their head in the mouth of the dragon. In reality, many cops look to minimize any risk to their safety and seek out less stressful and dangerous assignments. I wholeheartedly respect that, as everyone should live their life as they see fit. It's another thing, though, to be a pelican and tell everyone that you're an eagle. My early partner was an eagle, and the rest of the birds knew it.

Metaphors aside, one of the most important things he taught me was the importance of taking control, because it is only when you are in control that you are safe. This principle sounds very basic and logical, almost like an introductory lesson that was taught to you in your early days in the academy. But after many years of wide-ranging service, I am still surprised to this day at the sheer number of officers who don't focus on taking control, who don't have the street skills to exert and establish control, or who don't have the sense of what being in control really means.

A basic factor in control is establishing and implementing your will upon a person or situation. A dramatic example of exerting your will and gaining control occurred while I was still on probation and working with the "eagle". One night, while on patrol in the Van Nuys Division, we heard a broadcast over the police radio regarding a family dispute and a so-called "415" fight, which refers to California Penal Code section 415 (disturbing the peace) - what we generally refer to as a disturbance or as being disruptive.

While we were a few miles away from the scene of the disturbance, my partner decided that we should head there in any event to back-up the officers who were assigned to the call. At that time, Van Nuys Division was a large one geographically, so at times your nearest backup, if you needed one, could be a few minutes away. Seven or eight minutes are an eternity if you are attacked or fighting for your life.

As we drove to the scene, about three to four minutes prior to our arrival, we heard on the police radio that the assigned patrol unit plus an additional unit had arrived at the location.

Even this didn't deter my partner from responding. To me, despite the fact that there were already four officers at the scene, it was if he sensed that there was both a need for his skills and leadership, and a solid opportunity to train me, his rookie partner.

We arrived at the scene and exited our cruiser. We could hear screaming coming from the ground floor apartment where the disturbance originated. The front door of the apartment was open, and as we approached, the screams of a woman got louder and more belligerent. As a rookie cop on probation and with little practical experience, the scene that presented itself inside the apartment seemed to be a challenging one. The screaming woman was in her living room, holding in her right arm what appeared to be a six month old baby, and in her left, a jagged-edged broken beer bottle. She was obviously intoxicated, highly agitated and bleeding, and was more motivated to fight her equally drunk and bloody, but less combative, boyfriend situated across the room, than she was in caring for her infant.

The four uniformed officers who initially arrived at the scene stood shoulder to shoulder between the man and the woman. One of the officers was begging and pleading with the woman to drop the bottle and give him the baby. The more the officer spoke to her, the more disturbed and threatening she got. It was apparent that despite the large (and growing) police presence, the situation was in no way under our control.

Within a few seconds, however, my partner assessed the situation and threat level and said to me in a low, steady voice, "When I grab her, you grab the baby." That was it; no debate, no cajoling the woman, no fuzzy or complicated strategy, just a simple plan of attack focused both on the safety of a child incapable of protecting herself, and on an instantaneous short-circuiting of the tension in the room.

He quickly dashed over to the woman and with both of his hands, grabbed her left arm, the one holding the jagged beer bottle. Just as instructed, I stayed right on his heels and grabbed the baby from her before she could even figure out what was going on. My partner took her to the floor where she was handcuffed

63

with the help of the other officers. The male was also hand-cuffed, so, within seconds, the domestic dispute powder keg was diffused. Since they both assaulted each other, they went to jail and the baby was turned over to the L.A. County Children's Protective Services for safety.

I can recall, almost word for word, what my partner said to me as we later reflected on this incident: "The other officer didn't have control. She was drunk and not able to reason very well. The officer who was trying to talk to her was pissing her off even more. This whole thing was going bad. We had to take control. They stood around with their thumbs up their asses. Don't be like that. Be courageous and take control whenever you can." He was totally right. For this particular situation, I saw the master in action and learned that you must quickly assess the situation, commit to a decision, and take control.

When doing training sessions across the country, I make it a point to share with participants a little "control" test. Consider these five questions:

1. Is a handcuffed suspect under control?
2. Is a searched suspect under control?
3. Is a handcuffed suspect in the back of your police vehicle under control?
4. Is a suspect who has been searched and placed in a holding cell or interview room under control?
5. Are two handcuffed suspects whispering to each other under control?

As far as I am concerned, the answer to each question is "no". Here's why:

1. I have been involved in the search for a handcuffed prisoner on more than one occasion (fortunately, not my cuffs!);
2. Guns, weapons and contraband are found in the back of police vehicles, interview rooms and holding cells all the time. Someone missed those things in a search, or failed

to consider just how industrious a suspect can be in hiding items within body cavities;

3. Haven't you ever seen one of those humorous "Cops" television shows where the suspect leaves the scene driving the police vehicle with their legs or teeth?

4. See answer #2 (rubber gloves, anyone?);

5. Rest assured, they are not making plans to get together in the weight room or share a meal when they get to prison. You have no idea what they're saying, why they are talking or what they are planning. Just assume the worst.

If you believe what I'm saying, it should leave you a little on edge especially when dealing with any suspect in your custody. Pay attention, think proactively, and ask yourself pointed questions. Why is the suspect squirming around in the back of my police car? Why are the suspects trying to turn around and make eye contact with each other? Why are two of four gang members exiting their vehicle when you stop them, alone, for a mere traffic infringement? Why is the girlfriend of a suspect approaching you as you handcuff him on the ground? Sometimes you can't control everything. However, in your effort to focus upon gaining control over suspects and situations, you will develop into a much more safety-conscious and tactically sound officer. Habits can be either good or bad, so it makes sense to develop only good ones.

There is a certain universality to this lesson of taking control. Just as it applies to dealing with suspects and heated situations, it also applies to how you manage your career and even yourself. Viewed from this perspective, taking control means investing in your education and expanding your police muscles by pursuing unique and challenging assignments. It means taking the time to do something outside of your work to avoid burnout, and having the patience to deal with all people in a dignified way. And it means striving hard, always, to act with a high degree of character, class and self-confidence. Only when you exert and attain control in all facets of your work as a police officer will you be safe.

9

Follow The Piñata Principle

The great thing in this world is not so much where you stand, as in what direction you are moving.

OLIVER WENDELL HOLMES

Growing up as a happy young Mexican/American with lots of friends and a close family, I became quite good at whacking a piñata. As you may know, a piñata is usually made of paper mache, cardboard and sometimes a hardened clay material, like pottery. Normally brought out at children's birthday parties or family celebrations, a piñata is filled with candy and treats and is hung from the ceiling or a tree limb with twine. Children are then lined up, youngest to oldest, and one at a time take turns hitting the piñata with a stick, or "palo". To provide additional challenge, an adult pulls on the twine, therefore making the piñata move up and down as a child tries to make contact. The best part, of course, is when the piñata finally breaks and spills its contents. There is nothing quite like the glee of children scrambling on the ground for all the delicious treats that scatter there.

As I grew older and more competitive, it became a thing of pride to be the one who broke the piñata. On most occasions, it seemed to matter little which child would hit it first, as I was proficient in taking out piñatas due to my solid, but pint-sized, Mickey Mantle-like baseball swing.

Depending on the age distribution and composition of the group, adults organizing the piñata bash sometimes tried to even the odds to ensure all had a chance of cracking it open. Not only were the youngest given the first opportunity to strike away, but sometimes older children were blindfolded, spun around three times, and then pointed in the direction of the piñata. The combination of a slight case of the spins, a blindfold, and a dodging piñata often prevented an older kid from achieving success.

Somehow, though, I learned to counteract these handicapping techniques. After being blindfolded, whoever spun me around would normally leave me pointed in the right direction facing the now bouncing piñata. Because I was older – and had a reputation as a successful piñata buster - the person pulling the twine would do so even more violently, something which actually helped me.

Rather than wailing away desperately, I used my sense of hearing to detect the distinct whirring sound of the piñata and its twine disturbing the air around itself. I would key in on the sound, give a decent first whack to make contact, then immediately give a second follow-up whack which often was all that was required to expose the guts of the piñata. My first strike was based on sound, my second based on the feedback from the first. They key was, though, to be pointed in the right direction. If a parent blindfolded me and pointed me in just any old direction, I would have looked like a fool walking around with a blindfold, flailing my palo. I would still be wandering around to this day looking to nail my first piñata.

In a very real way, my attitude in solving gang crimes is to use the Piñata Principle: first get pointed in the right direction, and then use your instincts, senses and experience to navigate towards your goal.

Getting the initial direction you need is often the first and most difficult challenge you'll face. For a variety of reasons, people may be hesitant to help you solve a gang crime or help you establish your bearings. They may be afraid of revenge or retaliation from gang members which is a very real concern and commonplace occurrence. They may not want to be bothered or inconvenienced by the criminal justice system itself, or perhaps have even been "victimized" by it in the past. If you haven't invested the energy to develop a rapport with the community or if you go about your police work with many character flaws in tow, they simply may not trust you or want you to succeed. And many times, people just don't want to pay the price for getting involved. But if you are effective at what you do and are perceived as genuine, you can get people involved even in only a small way.

Then there is the issue of evidence. Despite what television viewers are led to believe, major crimes don't get solved within a 60-minute time span as they do on the top-rated show CSI. Real investigators don't pull up in brand new $40,000 Chevy Tahoes, alongside beautiful women displaying ample cleavage, then proceed to collect a mountain of physical evidence that always connects the perpetrator to the heinous crime. I wish it were the case, but it just doesn't work that way in the real world.

In order to solve a crime, police officers and detectives must first be pointed in the right direction. Physical evidence increasingly allows us to do this, but in the violent world of working gangs where crime scenes are often anything but pristine, the input of people, however limited, is essential.

I have always felt that knowing something is better than not knowing anything at all. If someone wants to tell me something and not get dragged into court, then I'll ask them to tell me and let me worry about court later. Again, it's like I'm blindfolded and I ask them to simply point me in the right direction and let me use my instincts and experience to take me the rest of the way.

One night when I was working the gang detail in our Newton Street Division, a gang-related shooting occurred. Someone from the local Blood gang was shot by a rival and my partner and I were called to the scene just a few minutes after it happened. As you can imagine, the victim's three fellow gangsters were very upset about their homie getting shot, especially since his chances of survival looked slim as the fire department ambulance transferred him to the local hospital's trauma unit.

Normally, when I was just passing through their neighborhood, I would stop and "play" with these gangsters by having a conversation with them or making a wise crack about someone's shoes or clothes. It was just another strategy I employed to develop relationships and sniff out information. While I was familiar to them, on the occasion of this shooting the last thing these three gang members would be in the mood for was my typical Don Rickles act. I knew as I stepped onto the curb where they were standing that I shouldn't to try to reason with them, "gain rapport" or cool them off. I knew better. I did, however, try to appeal to their emotions.

My assumption was that the suspects in this shooting were from one of two Crip gangs that I knew were warring with this Blood set. One Crip gang claimed territory immediately to their west, while the other immediately to their south. In a casual but concerned manner, I approached them and said, "Look, the guys who did this are chicken-shit. My partner and I have four hours to kill before we go off duty. We are going to go and mess with someone. Now, we can go across Central Avenue and mess with them fools, or we can go across Slauson Avenue and mess with them fools. I really don't want to waste my time".

The "OG" – original gangster - of this group looked at me and subtly pointed his right index finger toward Slauson Avenue, indicating to me which rival gang had committed the shooting. As we prepared to drive off, I decided to press my luck, so I asked, "And what kind of ride would I want to mess with?" Again, OG gave me the information I needed to orient myself: "A green Chevy."

While we didn't apprehend the suspects on that evening, we eventually did so and brought them to trial. Our condition of blindness at the outset was improved by the cooperation of some gang members who wanted retribution, and they were instrumental in helping us avoid wasting time or wondering aimlessly, "who did it?". When you are in the field pursuing a criminal, you'll rarely be handed the whole story, but you don't need it. All you need is a small push in the right direction, and the confidence to let your experience, training and intuition take you the rest of the way.

So, where's that piñata?

Lessons From A Gang Cop

SECTION TWO
Character

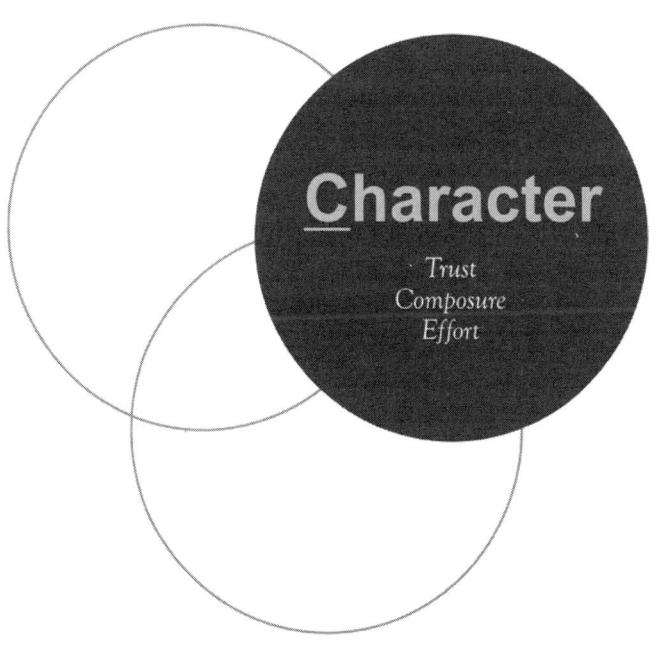

Character

Trust
Composure
Effort

10

Being a Character is Not Having Character

Who you are speaks so loudly I cannot hear what you say.

RALPH WALDO EMERSON

The finest police officers I know ultimately want to be recognized for the sum total of the qualities and values that make them who they are. Being known as someone who is bigger, badder, more belligerent or distinctive in some other visible way is, in my experience, not necessarily a good thing.

From 1982 to 1986, when I was with the LAPD's Detective Support Division-Gang Unit, I was given a list of unsolved crimes and a bright yellow Plymouth Fury police car that no one else wanted to drive.

I headed for the gang turf ruled by more than a dozen gangs in our city's Newton Street and South Los Angeles neighbourhoods, and later I discovered that I earned the nickname of "Pacman", after that famous little yellow blob of arcade game fame. One day a local resident told me, "Do you know what they call you? Pacman, because of that yellow monster that eats everything up." While I thought the imagery of the nickname was amusing, I really didn't like being called that name. I didn't let the gangsters know that I didn't like it because they would have been relentless in using it against me to piss me off. I acted as if it was just what they called me. No big deal. But deep down I didn't like the name because I wanted the gangsters to know me as "Moreno", because that's who I was. I was the gang cop who had worked at developing the various qualities and attributes that made me effective in working gangs. I wanted them to know me by my name as the guy who got things done and took care of business; me, Moreno, not some silly video game cartoon character whose purpose was to avoid the ghosts and eat the little white pills.

Unfortunately, the nickname stuck and before long, my partner and I began hearing shouts of "Pacman!" when we pulled into South Los Angeles neighborhoods. The nickname was so popular that gang members even began yelling Pacman at the sight of uniformed patrol officers. I was amused to later learn that after the movie *Colors* was released, other cops wanted to use a similar type of police car (there were at least two others in our fleet), and were flattered by gangsters calling *them* Pacman. To me, it was as if my fellow officers felt cool, legitimate or accepted when they were called by a nickname, especially one as unique as Pacman. What was even funnier were other cops, who didn't know me or my story that well, claiming that they were the original Pacman!

My point is that it's better to be acknowledged for the total sum of your character and your work, rather than the folklore surrounding a nickname. It is also better to earn a reputation through your good deeds, rather than trying to draw attention to your work by purposely positioning yourself as a unique, outlandish, loud or "Hollywoodesque" cop. If you work long and hard enough - and if you produce results - you will eventually get acknowledged for who you really are.

Just because everyone knows who you are doesn't necessarily mean that you're good at what you do. I'm sure you know some cops who are real characters. They always are, or attempt to be, at the center of attention. For the most part, they are "great guys". The question is, are they any good at what they do? Are they all frosting and no cake? *Are* they a character - a wise guy - or do they *have* character? There's a big difference.

If you have made a conscious choice to work in the demanding world of gangs, you need to be concerned about developing a meaningful and genuine reputation. If gangsters sense that your outward actions and demeanor are contrived, then you'll get no respect from them. And with no respect, you cannot be effective. Whatever their many faults, gang members are very streetwise and generally good at reading people. Like a dog that can sense fear, gang members can sense a manufactured character, and you'll pay the price.

What a gang member thinks of you determines how he'll deal with you. Your actions, insight and behavior establish your reputation with them. Initially, a gang member will assume that you are like all other cops in the way you act and think. They will believe that you are naïve with respect to gang life. They will believe that they are much smarter and tougher than you. Until they get to know you, they will treat you like they treat all other cops.

Over the years, I have spoken to countless gang members regarding their perceptions of police officers in general, and certain police officers in particular. Time and time again they tell me that street knowledge is very important to them in terms of how they view you, something which they judge in your conversations with them. Even the youngest baby gangster knows that a wet-behind-the-ears recruit, fresh out of the academy, will call everyone "sir" or "m'am", so it's no wonder that they treat rookies with little respect. They can also tell as much about you by your speech and vocabulary, as how you treat people.

My style or method was to be easygoing and pleasant until we had to get down to business. My reputation was that of a cop who didn't sweat the light stuff. I didn't waste my time with small time things like tickets and misdemeanor warrants. But if you were wanted for a serious crime, I was tenacious about catching you, and gangsters knew – and respected – that.

Now, I was very safety conscious, but I was also friendly yet sarcastic in a down-to-earth manner. I wasn't defensive or overly suspicious, and dealt with gangsters in an approachable fashion. I also joked around a lot. I guess to them, I was a fun guy as far as cops went, so if they were going to have to deal with cops anyway, they might as well deal with one they liked.

What most surprised me was the fact that those I primarily dealt with in my early years on the LAPD - Crips and Bloods - were primarily black. But I was clearly a Mexican-American, so we really didn't have anything in common. That's when the revelation struck me that with gang members, it's not what you are, it's who you are that determines if they'll give you the time of day. Sure, gang members in general don't like cops, but they will deal with you, no matter your skin color, nationality, gender or appearance. It's a matter of how you conduct yourself. You're judged on your gang knowledge, street smarts, courage, fairness and logic, the latter being very important to gang members who are trying to survive out on the mean streets.

Acting with character is not just about getting information and being effective, operationally speaking. A good reputation amongst the individuals you are policing can also save your life. I can vividly recall an example of how my good reputation got me out of a bad jam and probably saved my life. Back in 1984, I was assigned to the Los Angeles County Jail and worked alongside Los Angeles County Sheriff's deputies within the jail's gang unit. I had my own desk and worked with some of the most knowledgeable cops I've ever had the pleasure of working with. I was the lone LAPD officer working in the jail, and spent my days interviewing gang members to determine their affiliations and gather valuable intelligence that inevitably floated around the institution.

One day, on an information gathering mission, I walked down a hall and into module #4800, the Crip module, where the most hardcore and violent Crip gang members where housed. Soon after I arrived, a group of about 20 Crips left the module, shackled together, and were being escorted away to see their visitors in another part of the jail (an event that most prisoners looked forward to).

I went about my business, and when I was preparing to leave the module, I began to hear a roar from the adjacent hallway that seemed to get louder and louder. I was still deep in the module, near a booth where a deputy was stationed to watch inmates, perhaps some 25 feet from the exit. As the noise continued to grow in intensity, Crip gang members suddenly began storming into the module. They were angry and cursing vehemently, and the pack was coming straight at me. Instantly, I realized that these were the same gang members who, moments earlier, had been escorted away to see their visitors. As I later learned, one of the gangsters disrespected the escorting deputy and for punishment, the deputy decided to return them to their module without getting to visit with their wives, girlfriends and families.

About ten of the Crips were inside the module blocking the door to the hallway with more coming in. The rest were being unshackled in the hallway, soon to add to the horde. One of the bigger gangsters then said, "Fuck these pigs … we're going off!" They were going to riot.

He then saw me, standing in the middle of his module, without any form of protection. With a look of sheer menace and hatred, he said simply: "Look at this. What the fuck are you doing here, pig?"

It would be an understatement to suggest that I was stuck in a very bad place. I had no way of predicting that this was going to happen, so I had made no defensive preparations. Since the incident happened so soon after the inmates were escorted from the module – and because no one knew I had entered the module – I was completely exposed and vulnerable, no match for more than a dozen Crips whose emotions were inflamed and who were very much intent on destruction. Even the deputy in the module booth couldn't see me and therefore summon help.

About the only thing I could have done was run back towards the deputy's booth and bang on the door. The deputy probably wouldn't have let me in because then he would have been in jeopardy, but at least he could call for help. The Crips kept coming in the door from the hallway, and began to circle their prey – me. I prepared myself for the inevitable whack from behind and cursed at myself for allowing this predicament to happen. I never thought that I would make the six o'clock news as a helpless hostage in a riot at L.A. County Jail, with my life hanging in the balance.

Surprisingly, however, a gang member who knew me from the street stepped up and said, "Let him through. He ain't got nothing to do with this shit. He's alright." The sea of blue Crips parted and I walked calmly to the hallway, and to my freedom. It was a totally unexpected turn of events. As it turned out, the gang members had a minor disturbance in the jail; no one was hurt and there were no hostages.

A few days later, I spoke with the gang member who saved my ass back in the module. I asked him why he did it. He told me that he knew that I was "OK" and that I wasn't a prick. He also pointed out, however, that if I had previously acted like a hot-head on the streets and pissed people off with attitude, his boys wouldn't have thought twice to teach me a little lesson in the module. In his mind, I was just a cop who did his job the right way and didn't try to screw over people. I was a stand-up guy who treated people firmly but with respect. While I had few direct dealings with this individual in the past, he nonetheless formed a distinct opinion of me from both watching me work in his neighborhood for several years, and from listening to what his fellow gangsters said about me. His perception of my character, ultimately, was what motivated his action to save me from great harm in the jail module.

No off-the-shelf insurance package could have provided me with that level of protection either; it was earned, as I have said elsewhere in this book, one inch at a time, one street corner at a time, one interview at a time, one arrest at a time. That's the thing about character; you can't fake it, but must earn it. And once you do, you must follow the lesson in the old Quaker saying, "Let your life speak". Hopefully, it will do so, much more clearly and compellingly than what other "characters" have to say.

11

Celebrate Victory With Dignity

Mental toughness is many things. It is humility because it behooves all of us to remember that simplicity is the sign of greatness and meekness is the sign of true strength. Mental toughness is Spartanism with qualities of sacrifice, self-denial, dedication. It is fearlessness, and it is love.

VINCE LOMBARDI

Those who know me well know that I value dignity and consider it one of my most important law enforcement "tools". To many, this may appear to be quite contradictory since the gang culture is so violent and unrestrained. How can acting with decorum possibly benefit you when dealing in an environment where other human beings would rather see you dead or at least, greatly diminished? Good question.

Growing up, my concept of dignity was first learned and reinforced in the world of sports, specifically professional football. Back in the early 1960s, whenever Jim Brown of the Cleveland Browns or Jim Taylor of the Green Bay Packers scored a touchdown, they simply turned and casually handed the ball to the referee. They acted with dignity and humility, and I considered them powerful examples. There was something so compelling to me about a six-foot-two-inch, two hundred and thirty-two pound fullback like Brown remaining so calm and composed after he clashed and dashed his way to the goal line, escaping the clutches of much bigger men. The gesture of simply giving the ball to the referee was indicative to me of a person who was at the top of their game and was very secure in their ability. He had just scored a touchdown. That was his job and that is what he expected of himself. He wasn't surprised, shocked or startled by his accomplishment. He didn't try to outshine the work of his teammates who also had to do their jobs in order for him to get there in the first place.

I have been around talented officers who have lived weeks or months off of a high-profile arrest, celebrating incessantly about their achievements. Perhaps you know officers like this, too; the ones who gloat, brag and carry on about some caper as though anything others did was unimportant, as if they were God's gift to law enforcement; the ones who can somehow transform a routine 3-pound trout catch into a heroic 942-pound, 8-hour blue marlin capture.

If I have been involved in the arrest of a murderer, I'm not the type who high-fives everyone, throws confetti or shoots off fireworks. I have inner pride in my accomplishment, but the bottom line is that I expected to catch the suspect. I always expect to catch the suspect. That satisfaction, although real, is also fleeting. The more success I have, the more I want.

When the people I supervise in my unit make great arrests and do outstanding work, I don't outwardly make a big deal about it. The detectives in our unit have come to learn it's not that I don't admire or appreciate their work. The greatest compliment I can give them is that I expect outstanding work and success from them.

Recently, two of our investigators made contact with the lieutenant of another division within our department whose unit – a relatively new one – was responsible for monitoring and investigating certain gangs within a particular portion of the city. They had initiated a task force operation that was funded to last approximately two years, and we offered our services to help them start in. He blew our people off. He had all the help that he needed ... "thanks, but no thanks" was his curt response.

Soon thereafter, two members from a gang the unit was responsible for monitoring committed a robbery. The lieutenant and his unit weren't aware of this crime and therefore weren't investigating it. But we were. We made a courtesy call to the lieutenant to inform him of the crime, and that we were actively assisting the detective to arrest the suspects.

We discussed this case within our unit, including the initial attitude of the lieutenant towards members of our squad who were offering their assistance and support. We knew that we had to bring the suspects in, both to ensure justice and also to show the lieutenant that our unit performed and could be a huge asset to his.

A day later, our squad conducted a surveillance operation in south central Los Angeles looking for the suspects and their vehicle which had an "armed and dangerous" warning flagged on the license plate number within our computer system. We sat all day with no sign of the suspects and decided that we should start to pack it in. Suddenly, however, the wanted vehicle pulled up across the street from the residence we were watching with the two wanted suspects inside. As they walked across the street to the driveway of the residence, our officers pulled up and arrested them before they knew what had hit them. They were taken into custody without incident.

Now came time to transport them to the police station for processing - the same station where the rude lieutenant and his team happened to be based. The sight of us pulling up to the station was quite impressive - six undercover cars with two robbers plus their vehicle in tow! We exited our unmarked police cars with our arrestees and took them into the station under the watchful eye of the officers who worked at the station. We were professional, humble and mature in our demeanor. No high-fives. No bragging. No gloating. As a close knit unit of officers, we knew that making arrests like this was simply what we were supposed to do. That was what we were paid for. That was what we, and the community-at-large, expected of us.

As important, we knew that our professional demeanor would foster respect from the other officers with whom we would eventually have to work again. Sure, it was a real nice arrest, and to me, it felt just like I imagined it would feel to quarterback a football team on a 6-play, 90-yard touchdown march in the fourth quarter of a crucial playoff game. But what was most satisfying wasn't the actual arrest, but my team's action of simply handing the referee the ball, acting like they expected to catch the suspects all along. This act alone ensured that they will get the support and respect from their peers when they need it in the future.

Let it also be said that acting with dignity is not some superficial thing; it can actually save your life, as it did for me in the L.A. County Jail. Dignity is an essential law enforcement tool. Nothing so effectively fires up the resentment of a gang member than celebrating their arrest in their face or in front of their peers. Once in a while, it may be necessary or appropriate, but normally it will make things worse.

In my experience, gang members will respect the fact that you caught them in the commission of or after a crime – after all, you were both just doing your job. But they will most assuredly plan their revenge, if you rub salt in their wounds. Think about it: a gang member in prison has nothing but time on his hands, time that is often spent planning an escape, the perfect prison-built weapon, a future crime, or their vengeance against someone who has wronged them. So, dignity is also about officer safety. Celebrate your victories with dignity, and try not to act as if it is your first touchdown.

12

Focus On The "A" For Effort

I didn't want a spectacular play once in a while, I wanted a solid play every time.

JOHN MADDEN

In the world of policing, as in life, it's impossible to perform at peak levels at all times. You'll have bad days and you'll have great days, and they will likely be interspersed with a whole bunch of ordinary days where not much happens. You'll have high-energy days where your mind, body and spirit are locked and loaded, and you'll have the dog-tired days where all you can do is coast. You are allowed to have bad days, and you are allowed to pace yourself.

Look around you in any high performance endeavor and you'll notice that those who are at the "top of their game" all have one thing in common: they are consistently solid performers who put forth the effort day in and day out.

Henry Aaron hit 755 home runs in his 23-year career, an average of 33 per year, and never had a 50-plus home run season, something which has happened 13 times since 1998. Gordie Howe scored 801 goals in a 26-year career, yet never scored more than 50 in a season, a milestone that often defines a "great" NHL scorer. And Cal Ripken Jr. – who never set the world on fire with his batting conquests – is perhaps regarded as the world's most consistent and hardworking athlete *ever*, having produced solid results in 2632 consecutive games.

Sure, these athletes had many great single-day performances, and perhaps many more bad days. But the point is that consistently solid performance brought about by honest effort - and not intermittent sparkling performances - is what defined their greatness.

Returning to our world, your overall value consists of the sum total of your knowledge, effort, dedication and achievements along the way. If you are able to operate at a sufficiently strong level in all these areas over a long period of time, you'll be judged as consistently effective. You'll be considered a "solid performer".

I supervise a unit whose prime mandate is to help other LAPD detectives hunt down dangerous wanted criminals. These criminals are the worst of the worst, and our daily surveillance and field work is the stuff action cop shows are made of.

As a supervisor, it's my job to go out and find the most qualified individuals to work within our unit. Out of 9,000 officers on the Los Angeles Police Department, I have to find the very best cops to fill our 12-person unit. The ideal person is one who is dedicated, effective, resilient, knowledgeable and of good character. The ideal person is smart and savvy, and has the nerve to confront and capture a criminal once they are uncovered. We are an elite unit, and others know that you must come here and work hard and play tackle, not touch, football.

Recently, to fill a vacancy on my unit I recruited a female detective whom I knew had the right stuff. She is a very talented individual and has a reputation of being a dedicated, hard working cop. An added plus was that she is a real positive person who has a good influence on the morale of the unit. She is neither a whiner nor a complainer.

Once she joined our unit, she fit in right away. Our unit works in such a way that when any individual team gets close to one of their targets, we all go along for the capture, largely for officer safety purposes. This means that if another team gets close, the other teams have to drop what they're doing to lend a hand. She is always there to help and is very good tactically in the field. The only problem (in her mind) was that after a few months, she had yet to make a "big catch" like many other teams in our unit had done. While she tracked down a murder suspect and led the concerned detectives to his location for the arrest, she wasn't happy with that because she didn't do the take down. I sensed that she was getting frustrated and unhappy with her performance relative to her peers, so we sat down and had a chat.

I told her that I wanted her in our unit because of the type of cop, and person, she was. I told her that I didn't bring her into our unit because we needed more arrests or because we needed a woman on our squad. I wanted her because her skills, approach and character would compliment our unit, and because I knew she would be very successful.

I then told her that all I expected from her was an honest and consistent effort: "When I look over at you, I just want to see that you're trying". She had the knowledge and the talent, but it wouldn't mean anything if she didn't put forth the effort.

She thanked me sincerely, and at that moment I believe she realized that this whole thing was simple. Just give an honest effort, do good deeds, and success will follow. The classic quote applies here: "As you shall sow, so shall you reap".

I believe that by releasing her pressure valve that was stuck on "I haven't performed", it allowed her to be more effective. Indeed, about a month later, while checking a possible location with her partner, she saw a homicide suspect and swooped him up without a problem. I was out of town doing a lecture at the time but I called her to congratulate and remind her that all I expected was an honest effort, because that is what produces success.

I have proven this principle to myself time and time again when coaching amateur athletes. I have coached in several sports and have had the pleasure to work with hundreds of kids eager to perfect their sporting skills. Occasionally, especially when coaching so-called competitive "club" teams, I have encountered youth whose skills were head and shoulders above the rest; youth who could control a game on their talent alone. While I respect any young person with that level of mastery of a game, I hold equal, if not greater respect, for the child with fewer raw skills but who brought to the playing field an overabundance of effort and a record of consistent performance.

As a law enforcement officer that deals with gangs, if you can invest high quality effort and do so consistently over a sustained period of time, you'll earn the distinction as a "solid performer", and it's what people will just come to expect of you.

More importantly, it's what you will come to expect of yourself.

13

What Goes Around, Comes Around

Results are what you expect. Consequences are what you get.

ANONYMOUS

For those of us who have worked in the front lines around gangs and gang activity, we know first hand that gang life is a dangerous and violent existence.

The fundamental nature of gang culture is for one set of gang members to be aggressively at odds with their enemies - rival gang members - so as to protect turf, neighborhood boundaries, reputations, girlfriends and drug markets, among other things. In the absence of defined rules of conduct, violence is the tool of choice for gang members to protect all that is dear to them. Gang members have little respect for others and usually lack the social skills to handle adversity or conflict without resorting to violence. Violence in the gang world is a badge of honor. The greater your propensity for violence, the more valuable you are to your gang.

If you were to look at the traditional turf-oriented street gang, you'd find a group of individuals bound together by common interests, usually criminal in nature, but based on a neighborhood or geographic bond. If gang members stayed in their own neighborhoods and only ventured out to conduct personal or legitimate business, there would be no gang warfare. Everybody would have a corner of the world that they would call home, and they'd all be happy.

87

That's not the reality of gang life, however, because gang members don't stay in their own little corner of the world. Just as they disrespect society and its rules in general, they disrespect each other, thus perpetuating persistent gang warfare. They need to get in the last blow, to launch the last assault, to top their enemy's last violent act.

Enter you, the gang professional, into the middle of all this. There is resentment on the part of the gang member for you as you are an outsider. You're an outsider because you aren't part of their neighborhood. "You don't belong here....what goes on here is none of your business", you're told. To them, you are essentially an intruder who only works there and doesn't have a personal stake in or understanding of the community and its people. You're also an outsider to the gang culture. You aren't part of the gang, and you certainly don't support it. You and your peers represent forces working against the gang to diminish its influence and its reach. This applies to cops, teachers, counselors, parole/probation officers, caseworkers or any other professional who seeks to prevent or suppress the growth of gang activity.

While you are definitely not on their side, the primary hatred and fear a gang member has is not for you, but his true enemy, the rival gang member. Most gangsters realize that you probably won't cold-bloodedly murder him, because they know that we play by the established rules of society, and are simply not capable of that level of unprovoked violence. The gangster knows that his rival gang member, in contrast, is perfectly capable of dispatching a bullet into his or his homie's head. This has been demonstrated over and over again and this, in large part, is what prolongs and stimulates gang warfare.

In a very real sense, then, you are not so much the enemy as you are a nuisance to the gang member. You are a part of their landscape and you are to be avoided, but you are not their principal threat. By the way you conduct yourself, however, you can readily elevate your "relationship" with the gang member from merely that of a persistent nuisance, to that of a threatening enemy.

I have learned over the years that gang members don't like being arrested and put in jail, but for the most part they understand that this is part of the game, the cost of doing business. If I drive by a group of gangsters, I may stop and conduct a search if my suspicions are aroused. I may stop and chat for a while, or I may simply drive by, wave and acknowledge their existence. I believe that if you asked a group of gangsters who know me to describe my approach, they would say that I am a cop that doesn't sweat the small stuff, that I am firm but fair. I pay particular attention to managing the fragile dividing line that separates being a nuisance from being an enemy, and this has helped me avoid many of the difficulties other gang cops experience.

If a gang member is wanted for a particular crime, my approach is different because I am going to take care of business. Recall the old Mafia saying popularized in movies like the *Godfather* and *Wise Guys*, "It's business, not personal." I try always to make them believe this, even when I truly enjoy locking up some hard core gangster. However pissed off they are for being captured, I always seek to leave them with the impression that "it's just Moreno doing his job."

Earlier, I stressed that your character must be genuine and you must let your good deeds, knowledge and true self speak on your behalf. Managing your place on the nuisance/enemy scale takes more than that, though. It takes perspective, and it takes objectivity.

No two gangsters are alike in their approach, demeanor, moral character, propensity for violence, willingness to support the aims of their gang, background or intelligence. Some gangsters are the baddest of the bad, capable of brutal violence that can question your faith in mankind. But others are tame, otherwise okay kids that perhaps have made some bad decisions and now are in over their heads.

When approaching gang members, I never make the mistake of treating them all alike. I never have believed, and still don't believe, that just because someone belongs to a gang and is sporting tattoos and colors, that he or she, the person, is always bad all of the time. I learned early on to separate the person from both their affiliation with a gang and their actual activity, and therefore crack down on only those who break the law. I remind myself that some young people find themselves involved in gangs for reasons that they cannot always control - violent peer pressure, lack of strong family role models, economic necessity or self protection - and not just because they perceive the gang lifestyle to be an attractive one full of long-term prospects for success.

Don't get me wrong. I don't really feel sorry for gang members because, after all, they are responsible for their actions and the decisions they make, however ill-advised. But I see gangs and their dynamic in shades of grey, rather than in black and white. I do not treat all gang members *equally*, but do so *equitably*, and there is a world of difference between these two concepts. This perspective allows me to focus on taking care of business for those who deserve orange jumpsuits, cavity searches and months of prison food, rather than treating all gangsters alike and therefore fitting their concept of being a "punk-ass" cop.

There is an old saying I like that underscores the issue of prejudice and the dangers of a single-minded perspective: "If you give a child a hammer for Christmas, everything will look like a nail". To this day, I still see some gang cops swaggering like tough guys, intimidating gang members regardless of who they are and what they have actually done. Bad decision, because the job is already hard enough without you making it harder. If you bust heads, kick assess, get in the faces of gangbangers and generally cover them like a cheap dime store suit, you'll be remembered, and you'll be hated. They'll look for opportunities to take you down, to make your life, or the lives of your loved ones, miserable. Think about the risks involved for those of you who work in the community where you live. Think about your children who have to go to school and be out in the community. To a gang member who lives in the world of violent retribution, the maxim "what goes around comes around" is close to heart, and they practice it very well indeed.

While it is true that you might develop a lifelong enemy even when you are just minding your business and doing your job, you can minimize the enemies you make by being fair and using your head. Teachers, counselors and non-law enforcement professionals are in the same boat. You mustn't leave the impression that you are making a special project out of some gang member or his gang, even if you are. The easiest way to do this is not to get sucked into a personal rivalry. Taunting is one way for gang members to get under your skin or into your head, and they know that if they're not doing anything illegal, you are risking your career by trying to make something out of nothing. Don't make him believe that you are trying to run him out of your class, trying to put him jail or trying to deny his family certain benefits because of who he is.

A gang member is a marked man due to the nature of the game he is playing. We are not their primary threat. There is a good chance that bad things will come their way because that is part of the gangster's lifestyle. Countless times in my career, I've looked down at the bloodied and bullet-ridden body of a gang member and thought to myself, "what goes around really comes around."

14

Develop Their Trust in You

To be trusted is a greater compliment than to be loved

GEORGE MACDONALD

It has been said that "love makes the world go around". Maybe "trust makes the world go around" is more accurate.

Trust is the most important social lubricant there is. Trust is a necessary ingredient for any real relationship, whether in business, law enforcement or between any two people. When someone trusts you it means that you have demonstrated, by your conduct and past actions, that you will honor the other person's well-being and welfare when dealing with them. Because they feel safe and satisfied with your loyalty towards them, they hold you above others with whom they work or associate. They will help you get what *you want* as you give them what *they want*. And it is trust which makes it all happen.

In chapter 7, I wrote about the importance of knowing what motivates others. This is important, as it can help you determine how much you should trust others in your dealings. Who trusts you is equally important. If I have to deal with another law enforcement agency, I try to deal with a person with whom I have or can gain some prior knowledge. For example, if I require some information from the California Department of Corrections, the Los Angeles County Sheriff's Department or even another LAPD division, I won't just call and talk to whoever answers the phone. Rather, I will review the base of contacts I have cultivated over the years to see how I might best direct my call. If no suitable prospect exists, then I will network with my contacts and co-workers to see which of their trusted contacts I can access. If I trust you and your judgment, then I will trust whomever you trust. It is in this way that business gets done in an efficient manner.

There is no secret, underhanded or devious purpose for dealing with a trusted contact. The reason that a trusted contact is so important is that they care enough about you to be honest, thorough, accurate and go the extra mile for you. They probably realize that they are trusted by you and for that reason will work to maintain and enhance the trust. This effort on their part increases your appreciation for them and enhances your relationship with that person. It's as if they are continually making emotional deposits in your "trust account", from which they will be able to make withdrawals in the future.

Trust is an intuitive concept and most people get it in terms of its sheer value, but it is difficult in practice because it takes more than just words, a smile or the request, "just trust me". You can't fake your way to trust any more than you can fake your way to being an effective police officer. It takes certain actions and genuine behavior over a sustained period of time to earn the trust of another.

In the business of working gangs, a lot of information is sensitive and confidential. Many times, things are not designed to be known by the general public or law enforcement. The effective gang cop is able to go into a neighborhood and extract information, information that was never meant for him or anyone else to know. That type of cop is the one you want to be and the one you want to include in your personal network of trusted contacts. That type of cop also, unfortunately, is the one who often gets used by people wishing to short-cut their way to the top.

I will draw an analogy regarding you and what other people might want: your knowledge. Imagine an attractive young woman sitting alone at a bar. She is approached by various guys in the bar who express interest in her. They attempt to impress and make her feel special in order to gain her interest. Their ultimate goal is to gain her trust, so that one of them may become the chosen one. The lucky guy may succeed in making her feel special, and leave her with the impression that their interaction will be beneficial to her in the long run (e.g., love and eternal happiness as husband and wife). Based on the guy's words and behavior, she may believe that her dreams of love and happiness are close at hand.

But the reality may be completely the opposite. As it turns out, the guy is not looking for love, but is really just some slime ball looking for some physical activity for the evening. He has no plans to carry on this relationship any further than that night. He won't care how she will feel tomorrow or the day after that. He won't care about the implications of their evening together, or her expectations, feelings or whatever else happens to her. He wants what he wants for his reasons and cares about nothing else. She will be deceived and lied to, all so that he can get what he desires. There will be no basis of trust, and no relationship can possibly ever form.

I can relate this scenario to a situation that I encountered a few years ago. No, I wasn't sitting alone at a bar getting hit on, but I was used and deceived because someone else wanted what I had. I got snookered.

An investigator from another agency contacted me and indicated that they were in the process of forming a task force to target a gang that I was quite familiar with. He was told that I knew this gang well, so he wanted to talk and compare notes. Hindsight being perfect vision, I should have smelled a rat in the beginning because this guy paid out compliments like a drunken lottery winner hands out tips, saying all of the nice things he'd heard about me. Since the gang in question was a common object of inquiry between his and my unit, he promised total cooperation and information exchange if I told him everything I knew about the gang. Our unit would be able to access his resources for our work, resources that we didn't have and could very much use.

He told me that he was in the process of completing an assessment report on the gang including key individuals and leaders and their particular activities. This is normal methodology as you want to know as much about your enemy as possible. I didn't know what he already knew about the gang so I gave him as much as I could. I took the bait and spilled my guts. I had a lot of information and answered his questions, and that led me to believe that he had done some homework on the gang.

At the conclusion of our interview, my counterpart left with enough information to complete a thorough assessment and provide his superiors with a sound base to launch the task force activities. He got what he wanted and left. I didn't hear back from him for a couple of weeks so I finally gave him a call. I wanted to see his final report because we were still dealing with the gang in question and I wanted the full picture of their involvement. I assumed that he had more information than just what I gave him, and would share it as he had originally promised.

I asked him about the report and he told me that I couldn't see it because it was "confidential".

I was shocked to say the least and snapped back, "Excuse me, it's 'confidential'?" Isn't the majority of your report the info I personally gave you?"

"Yeah, well, it's the way we have to do it because it's an ongoing investigation and my superiors want it done that way," he sheepishly explained.

"So let me get this straight," I jabbed. "You come to me for information, promise to share and collaborate, but now you can't even tell me what I've told you?"

"It's just the way things are done around here. I can't do anything about it," he added.

I was pissed at him because he had used me. I was also pissed at myself for not learning more about who he was or his possible motivation.

I'm sure that his report was great and that his superiors were pleased with amount of information that he developed. I'm also sure that he knew all along that I wasn't going to be able to see his final report. He just buttered me up to get the info and make himself look good. To me, he was the equivalent to the slime ball at the bar trying to pick up the pretty girl.

As I was preparing to say goodbye to my task force "colleague", I thought I'd pull his chain a little just to make him squirm and not be so sure of himself and his report. I said "How do you know that I was even telling you the truth?"

I could tell that he was puzzled by that remark, so he said, "Well, I heard that you knew these guys and I thought that I could trust you. Why would you lie?"

"Why would *you* lie! You'd better double check that information to make sure I was accurate," I shot back at him.

When I thought his blood pressure was really beginning to rise, I said goodbye, wished him luck and hung up.

Now, of course, my information was good and I am sure it was invaluable for his task force. The remark I made to him was my consolation prize, however. I wanted to make him think about what he did. Sometimes, we let little things pass and the perpetrator thinks that he got away with something. Not this time.

The thing was that if this guy approached me and had been honest about what he wanted and what he could and couldn't do for me, I would have given him everything he needed, with no expectation other than if he was ever in the position to do so, he might want to help me in the future. I guess to him I was just some dim witted LAPD cop whom he'd never need again. He disrespected me in the way he handled his business and needless to say, I would never trust this investigator again. His loss.

The point of this story is not to bitch and moan about how some guy from another agency lied to me and misappropriated information out of me. The point I am making is that by your past actions and deeds, you may be viewed by your contemporaries no different than that slime ball at the bar. You may not believe you deserve that reputation, but in life, as in the gang world, perception is reality.

The quote found at the start of Chapter 10 dealing with character sums it up well, "Who you are speaks so loudly I cannot hear what you say". Some cops say to others, "trust me", but their reputation as being untrustworthy and manipulative has a funny habit of preceding them sometimes. They may not know it or choose to admit it, but their inability to build and substantiate trust in others puts them on the fast track to nowhere.

Within law enforcement, the terms collaboration, co-operation, teamwork, sharing and exchange are commonplace, but mean nothing without trust. The more that people, cops, friends, gangsters, superiors, co-workers and citizens alike trust you, the more successful you will be. Your conduct and interactions with others will establish their level of trust in you. If you are unselfish and give something in return for nothing in the spirit of goodwill, you will establish trust. Unless individuals work together in earnest with others, however, trust remains only a concept. Regrettably, sometimes the very culture of policing, with its inherent competition for title, rank and commendation, short circuits the trust development mechanism and leaves us all poorer for it.

It takes time, effort and sacrifice to establish your personal network of trusted people. Trust supersedes rank, agency, job title, age, gender, ethnicity, profession, religious beliefs and just about any other factor you can think of. The wise words of Albert Einstein perhaps make the point best: "Every kind of peaceful co-operation among men is primarily based on mutual trust and only secondarily on institutions such as courts of justice and police". Whom you trust, and vice versa, has such a major impact on what happens to you in life and in law enforcement, that it pays to develop the skills and attitude necessary to develop it.

Trust me.

15

What A Leader Does

To be a leader, you must be honest with yourself and know, as a leader, you are like everyone else, only more so.

FRANKLIN D. ROOSEVELT

For most of the gangs I've worked over the years, there has existed no formal rank structure or hierarchy of titles as is found in every police agency. Just as an individual has to earn his way into the gang, he or she has to also earn and cultivate respect and influence amongst other gang members. Certain factors go into determining how much influence or "juice" someone has within the gang. The following are some of the more significant factors that are used to judge and situate a gang member within the overall gang structure:

Background: Where are you from? If you come from a family where your three older brothers are from the same gang, that's good. If you are new to the neighborhood and little is known about you, that's bad.

Age: The older you are, the more respect you "should" get (this is the seniority factor).

Experience: How long have you been in the gang? Have you done time in prison? Have you been involved in incidents or situations involving rival gangs, the police or the justice system? Do you share your experiences with others?

Reputation: What do people think when they hear your name? Are your peers glad to have you around? What effect do you have on those around you? What does the enemy think of you?

Loyalty: How loyal are you to the gang? How have you proven your dedication? What priority does the gang have in your life? How many tattoos do you have to show dedication to the gang?

Judgment: What kind of decisions do you make? Can you make a decision? Can you make good decisions?

Efficiency: Can you do what you're told? Do you get results? Do you take care of what needs to be done?

Vision: Can you see beyond what's in front of you? Do you have a destination? Do you have a plan?

Courage: Do you react in a brave manner? Do you remain strong against unfavorable odds? Do you promote courage and confidence in others?

Unselfishness: Are others important to you? Do you protect others? Will you endure risk for the sake of others?

The gang leader is the person whose combination of these qualities gains him more influence and respect than others in the gang. It doesn't have to necessarily be only one person. You could see a group of gang members enjoying themselves at a park but if there are a lot of them, they may be broken down in separate groups. This is not unlike us at a promotion party or barbeque. In the case of the gang, the "veteranos" might be in one group because they are the upper hierarchy or "staff officers" of the gang.

Rarely does a major or entrenched gang have just one leader. Most often, there are several leaders within the gang who show respect to each other and have established a workable protocol when dealing with each other. That's why as you learn and deal with your gangs, you need to know the influential and significant members and be able to distinguish them from the rank and file.

Indeed, it is a definite advantage for a gang to have more than one leader. It is expected for gang members to be hurt and killed by their enemies and to also be incarcerated. When a death or arrest of a gang member creates a vacuum, someone who has already established his credentials and is respected must step in and close the hole. Someone has to take up the slack on behalf of the gang in order to keep things running smoothly. When the leadership dynamics of a gang change, so too does the gang, much like any other organization.

In most gangs, you will also have members who are exceedingly violent, more so than the norm. This extreme propensity for violence may be due to drugs, mental illness, a twisted antisocial ego or a combination of the above. Those are the select few psychopaths who do damage to people and appear to have no sympathy or compassion for whoever gets in their way. There is no remorse and they just keep on doing evil deeds and hurting others. They are the worst of the worst. In the gang world of crime and violence, they are the "hitmen", the "shooters" or the "muscle". Even their fellow members tread lightly in their presence. Their own kind will give them a lot of room so as to minimize contact and the possibility of something going wrong. A person who is violent, quick tempered, impulsive and highly unpredictable is someone to keep at arm's length.

But know this: even the most violent member of the gang isn't necessarily a leader. His fellow gangsters fear him, but they certainly do not respect him in the traditional sense of the word.

On a few occasions in my career, I've had gangsters snitch on one of their own members because he was in a violent and "possessed" mode, and was just too unpredictable for even their own kind to sleep well at night. Once I was approached by a gang member who wanted to give me some information. Prior to his approach, this guy had never given me the time of day but now he had a problem, a real big problem, and he needed a solution. People in distress in the gang milieu often represent the best source of information because their safety or that of a loved one depends on it. I was listening.

According to my new informant, one of the OG's (original gangsters) in his crew was smoking "sherm" (PCP laced cigarettes) excessively and was getting particularly violent, even with his own homeboys. And while the snitch could deal with the OG himself because he'd been around for a few years and had standing with the gang, he was concerned that the sherm-smoking maniac had his sights set on his little sister. The snitch made it known that he wasn't going to let that happen, but the OG persisted and interpreted the snitch's lack of enthusiasm as disrespect. To complicate matters, the OG was putting in a lot of work for his gang (committing acts of violence against the enemy gangs) so he was still considered a valued member of the neighborhood and an asset to the gang.

As the hardcore gangster was detailing his predicament in the interview room of my police station, I could see his eyes tearing up. I got up and left the room for a couple of minutes to let him compose himself, because I was afraid that if he felt too awkward or embarrassed, he might stop talking altogether. I let the gangster be a gangster and I left the room so he could maintain his dignity. When I returned, I sensed that he understood my face-saving departure, and he was ready to continue talking.

Now, I know that there are readers out there thinking, "Screw the bastard. That guy chose to be part of the gang life so let him deal with his own problems. He made his bed now let him lie in it." That's a reasonable objection, but I like the challenge of taking a violent maniac off the street before he does more damage. Besides, no matter how hardcore the snitch was, his younger sister didn't deserve to be the sex toy for some sherm-ed-out psychopath. As far as I was concerned, once the snitch left the room and continued in his gang life, he would eventually get what was coming to him. But at that moment, I was more concerned with saving the girl and taking the maniac off the street.

As I expected, the information provided about the OG was accurate. In one of his drug-induced acts of violence, he robbed a little mom and pop market a few miles away from his neighborhood. The informant gave me the day, time and location of the robbery. I verified that there was an armed robbery on that date at that market. I then contacted the detective handling the robbery case and provided him a picture of the maniac. The victim and witnesses picked him out of a photo line-up as the suspect who had robbed the market.

A few days later, we arrested the maniac without incident as he was hanging out with his homies. At the time, he didn't realize that he had been identified in the robbery and that there was a warrant for his arrest. He was eventually convicted and went to prison, and I am sure that many people in the community liked the fact that something bad happened to him and that he was gone. Make no mistake about it, though, he was no leader within the gang. While he was a significant member, he had no following or influence other than the fear and intimidation he imposed upon those around him. Indeed, a true leader in the gang would actually have worked to keep the maniac under control, channeling his skills and energy for the good of the gang.

When you assess the gang leadership factors listed earlier in this chapter, you'll notice that they are qualities of a good leader of any kind and in any domain, including mainstream society and law enforcement. So, the sum of the qualities that pushes a gangster to a leadership position within his gang (loyalty, vision, courage, etc.) are the same qualities that pushes a business executive to the top of his corporation or an athlete to the top of his game.

When you look at leadership in law enforcement, things sometimes get cloudy, however. Most cops would agree that with some degree of regularity, the promotional process seems to advance good students and qualified candidates, not true leaders. And while sending newly minted supervisors and leaders to a leadership academy may help with theory and concepts, they aren't necessarily going to become effective leaders in the full sense of the word.

In an environment where the less trouble, problems and complaints you attract, the better your odds for promotion, doing gang work does not put you on the fast track to advancement.

Working gangs places you squarely amongst criminals who arrogantly try to control the environment you work in. When working gangs, yours will be a world of violent confrontations, revenge and vendettas, and sometimes split-second life or death decisions. You will have to live with your decisions, and may even have to answer to and be judged by a tribunal or committee where not one member would be caught dead in your position or have the ability to execute the decisions you made. Unfortunately, that's the system of checks and balances within which we all must live.

But know this. You are not a leader because you passed a test. You are not a leader because you have a poster in your cubicle that talks about leadership. You are not a leader because you look good in your uniform. You are not a leader because your title says so. You are not a leader because you told your spouse and kids that you are. You are not a leader because you are sitting at the front of the squad room issuing directions. And you are not a leader because some other leader told you are one.

You are a leader if you care for others, and in doing so, take the lead. You are a leader if you assume the greatest risk. You are a leader if you give others confidence and incentive to do their job, and clear obstacles from their path so that they can be the best that they can be. You are a leader if you are prepared to roll up your sleeves and get as dirty as the most junior member of your squad. You are a leader if you are prepared to support your subordinates, even though you may lose the support of your superiors. Most of all, you are a leader if do the right thing, no matter what the circumstances may be and the pressures that may be placed upon you.

Another key to being a leader is recognizing the *other* leaders around you. Write that down and use it on your next promotional interview. I'll state it again: a leader is smart enough to recognize the other leaders around them.

If you are a new supervisor and get promoted or transferred to a new division, squad or watch, remember that there are people already working there, some of whom may have being doing police work from before the time you attended your first prom;

some of whom are already leaders in their domain. You have to realize that there are many levels of leadership - some above you, some below you - and that each level is important. To be a leader, then, you must be willing to be led. If you are effective in recognizing the other leaders and then getting them to support you, you've passed the first test in becoming a leader. But if you show up, push people around and decide things will be done your way, you will surely lose - people, morale, effectiveness and respect.

When I was working a neighborhood hard, I'd purposely seek out and talk only to the leaders of the gang. If I needed something done, a piece of information, or a feel for what was going on, I dealt with the leaders of the gang. I understood and respected the dynamics and complexities of the gang hierarchy. I let the gang leaders lead, and because I respected that, they rewarded me accordingly with solid and actionable information.

So, while working gangs is not necessarily a career accelerator, it does give you an in-depth lesson on leadership and the underlying qualities that constitute it. You will see leadership from both sides of the law and learn that leadership - or the lack of it – can be deadly.

16

Manage the Competitive Spirit

Competition has been shown to be useful up to a certain point and no further, but co-operation, which is the thing we must strive for today, begins where competition leaves off.

FRANKLIN D. ROOSEVELT

Law enforcement is among the most competitive professions in the world. To become a police officer, you must compete for that right. Each and every candidate who seeks a career in law enforcement must compete with dozens of others for every available position. And assuming you make it through the battery of intellectual, physical and psychological tests that are administered in the selection process, all you have earned is the right to enter the academy (where the real competition begins), and not an actual police job.

For those who are fortunate enough to have prior military experience, you may have an advantage at the academy, as it is an acute test of your maturity and competitive spirit. Similarly, experience in team sports may also help acclimate you to the rigors of the academy, as you will have already been exposed to competition, stress, teamwork, practice and individual responsibility.

While in the academy, you may be in competition with anywhere from 30 to 50 other candidates. I can remember my every day in the academy as a mental, physical and sometimes emotional battle. If my experience with the LAPD academy was representative of others across the country, anyone telling you that academy was easy or a walk in the park is lying.

It was difficult because you knew that your job depended on your performance. I had some real strong guys in my class and I can assure you that each and every one of us had bouts of uncertainty, lack of confidence and frustration. We were told to either give up or fight through the pain and adversity. We watched each other fight our own little battles which inspired us to push on, because if you didn't, you'd be eliminated from competition. And not only were you in competition with others, you were in competition with your own mind, will and spirit, forcing yourself to a new level of performance. Just like the marathon runner hitting the proverbial wall but pushing on through to the 26th mile, police academy is, for most, a test of mind over matter.

But successfully completing academy does not mean that the competition subsides. Upon graduation, you are placed in the field or in a custody facility. You are thrown into the fire and scrutinized against other recruits, trainees or probationers with the same level of experience as you. You are assessed on your ability to handle the job. You are under the microscope, analyzed by people who really don't want you to succeed past their level of competence. You are tested, cajoled and treated like a second class citizen. You are told by your supervisors the same old thing that was told to me 28 years ago, and to my predecessors 28 years before that, which goes something like this: "you recruits aren't as good as they were when I went through the academy!" That's simply not true, as good cops and bad cops went through police academy 50 years ago, and good cops and bad cops will go through police academy 50 years from now.

If you are fortunate and skilled enough to pass these tests, you then enter the real work of policing where even more competition is thrust your way. To get promoted to the rank of sergeant or detective, you must enter a competition. To get a good specialty assignment in narcotics or homicide, you must enter a competition. The competitive elements of policing never end, and I haven't even gotten to the part about serving the community and chasing bad guys who compete with you in a constant life and death struggle.

But working gangs is unique. If you fall into the trap of competing with others who work gangs, you may earn yourself a whole lot of problems. Rather than compete with other gang cops, you should compete with gang members and criminals. If your passion truly is working gangs, your focus should be on challenging yourself to learn and stretch, thereby making yourself more valuable to your police service and community. Comparing yourself with others whom you admire and respect in your profession is acceptable, as long as your focus is on understanding your weaknesses so that you can embrace their strengths, all in the spirit of constant improvement. Comparing for comparison sakes will only signal to others an ego or insecurity problem on your part and you may very well find your career stalling as a result.

In my experience, a focus on continual personal improvement provides an effective buffer from getting involved in petty competition, which can be exceedingly draining. The extent of competition in law enforcement is so marked in some agencies that it can transmute itself from a positive life force to a destructive cancer. I know, because I have developed enemies from time to time within my own peer group. In each instance, I believe I did nothing evil, underhanded or malicious. My newfound enemy didn't like me, I surmise, because he had compared himself to me and didn't like what he saw.

Reflecting on these instances, some common themes emerged. My enemies were usually people who recently began working gangs. They had a self-important view of themselves and their abilities. They weren't team players in the true sense. They were the kind of cop that would show up at a scene and exert their muscle and control. What helped me endure and succeed was my belief that my know-how was sincerely earned and honestly accumulated from gang members, knowledgeable peers and my own experience. However good or bad my enemies claimed I was, it mattered none to me because they could not possibly take away my knowledge and expertise.

Unfortunately, those who aggressively compete in the game of gangs fail to understand a fundamental reality: there is an infinite amount of gang knowledge to be obtained. Organized gangs have been in existence since the 1800s and the gang phenomenon continues to spread. Gang culture, trends and traits continually evolve, progress and mutate. Just as no one astrophysicist can possibly understand the entire structure of the universe, no one gang expert can understand everything there is to know about gangs. There are many gang experts, but there is no pre-eminent gang guru, simply because the gang is just too complex and diverse an organism. There is room for all of us to become brilliantly educated on gangs, because the subject is that immense. Stated another way, gang expertise is not constrained within a zero-sum game - what one has does not subtract from another's inventory.

If one of your fellow police officers is successful in aggravating you or your work relationships (and they will), it doesn't deter from who you are and what you have accomplished. Your knowledge, character and spirit cannot be taken from you, unless you allow it.

For years, I have had to deal with back biters who have tried to diminish me, but I am still here and getting better every day as a gang cop. At a gang meeting a few years ago, I grew tired of the snickering and snide remarks from a fellow police officer. In front of everyone, I said: "Don't compare yourself to me because you'll just make yourself crazy." I knew that he was a back stabber and operated by the dictum that if you discredit another, you will somehow elevate yourself above that person, regardless of their accomplishments. He believed that my knowledge, achievements and experience would mean nothing if he made people think he was better than me.

But it just doesn't work that way. This individual would have been much better off if he channelled that energy towards the growing gang problem in his area. The "enemy within" should motivate you to accomplish more, because there is nothing that succeeds quite like success. You can't dispute a great arrest, a thorough investigation or an amazing caper. You simply shut them up and short-circuit their nonsense by doing good deeds. Faced with a track record of your achievement, they will eventually give up and go away, and if they don't, they will end up looking like a fool. Backstabbers are the way they are because they are lazy and looking for a shortcut; so as long as you are dedicated to your cause, they will never match your dedication because that is a trait they know little about.

As you may reasonably conclude, being competitive is a double-edged sword. Competitiveness can be a noble quality when used wisely in the performance of your duties as a police officer. Being competitive keeps us in shape, and augments our ability to stay safe on the streets. But being competitive can also be a disaster when it is overused, particularly with respect to the competition we invariably engage in with our most vocal critic - the person in the mirror.

We all strive to live up to our expectations and those of our peers, family and friends. In a world where competition flows in the blood and becomes part of our DNA code, failing to meet expectations can be disastrous.

When I first started conducting training for law enforcement officers on gang issues, I was a bundle of raw emotions. If an attendee submitted a critical post-training evaluation, the blow to my psyche was quite staggering. Intellectually I knew that law enforcement officers were tough critics and difficult to win over, but such was the power of one negative response, that I paid no attention to the many positives.

For example, one day I provided training to the LAPD academy on the topic of prison gangs. I knew from the ebb and the flow of the program that the training day went very well, which was confirmed by the 39 glowing reviews from a total class of 40. But one negative evaluation stuck in my craw. It had such a negative and acutely personal tone that it was as if the officer had attended an entirely different class! To me, the nature of the commentary was such that he was clearly the "enemy" with a hidden agenda, who wanted to discredit me despite my best efforts to educate him on dangerous prison gang issues.

My mind began to reel. I tired to understand why this person didn't like me or my class. In lightning-like fashion, I reviewed the modules of my presentation to see where I may have lost him or his respect for the content I delivered. I began to punish and criticize myself subconsciously, and engaged myself in a competition I had no chance of winning because I could not turn back the hands of time.

A colleague I trusted snapped me out of my funk when he told me that he thought the program was great. This was the release valve I needed, as it immediately helped me focus on the 39 evaluations which were extremely complimentary. Whether the glass was half full or half empty was simply a matter of perspective and conscious choice - my choice. In teaching the class, my heart was in the right place as my goal was to help these officers stay safe and be more effective. Why in the world should I punish myself for that noble intention? Why in the world should I be so competitive with myself that I would focus on the single bad commentary in a sea of positive ones?

Perhaps you, too, have experienced this negative self-talk when presented with a citizen's complaint or a fellow officer's taunt, despite an otherwise fine track record as a police officer. The law enforcement competitive factor is what drives us to be competent, strong and able, and we tend not to accept criticism or failure well. Big goals and the motivation to be the very best you can be is fine, but we work in an extremely demanding and volatile world that delivers highs and lows. Failure and substandard results will occur, and sometimes they may be completely out of your control. But what always remains within your control is how you handle these failures, and the lessons you learn from the world of competition.

Remember that you are a human being attempting to help others who are experiencing serious problems. You are, however, a human that is more compassionate than most, more reliable than most and stronger than most. If something goes wrong, try to isolate the inherent lesson, and then focus on the overall effect you are producing in your life.

Competition is a powerful human dynamic, but despite the challenges and setbacks you may face, endure and remain loyal to yourself and those around you. That, folks, is what defines a real competitor.

Lessons From A Gang Cop

Commitment

Commitment

Vision
Passion
Belief

17

Do Something For Yourself Outside Your Work

The best and safest thing is to keep a balance in your life, acknowledge the great powers around us and in us. If you can do that, and live that way, you are really a wise man.

EURIPIDES

Working gangs is one of the most demanding kinds of police work. It's visible, violent, frustrating and intense. The expectations placed upon you to perform, both by your police counterparts and the community-at-large, are similarly challenging.

What's more, gang members tend to rub their gang culture and criminality in your face. Unlike drug dealers, prostitutes, bank robbers and white collar criminals that hide who they are and what they do, gang members, for the most part, don't. The street gang culture is such that to maintain their power to intimidate, recruit and protect turf, gang members blatantly impose their identity upon society. This gets your law enforcement neurons firing even faster, and pressures you to produce results, now.

For these reasons, and more, it's easy to become totally engrossed in gang work. But this can be dangerous, as you can quickly burn out. Effective police officers, especially gang cops, know that they must counterbalance the intensity of their work by taking periodic breaks from it. These time-outs allow you to gain a fresh perspective on your job, recharge your spirit and minimize the effects of burnout.

My former wife and I raised four wonderful children. One of the things I did in order to spend more time with my family, and give myself a break from work, was to coach. I coached youth soccer for over seventeen years, and also tried my hand at baseball, t-ball and basketball. Now, I wasn't a great coach and probably was never mistaken for Phil Jackson, Scotty Bowman or Jon "Chucky" Gruden, but the kids seemed to enjoy being around me, especially those who weren't getting the attention, love or reinforcement they needed from their parents. Coaching acted like a pressure release valve for me; it was my therapy, my escape, my hobby and my reward, especially since my own children were involved. Ironically, I found that I could go to work after a tough soccer game, drained from emotion, but be in a better state of readiness.

An unfortunate by-product of working some of the most violent streets of Los Angeles was that I had seen countless injured and dead children and teenagers. Some of the children I coached lived in and around these troubled communities and saw what I saw, but experienced it first hand. It was apparent to me as a father, and as a coach, that these at-risk kids were on the soccer field to have a good time, to escape the tension that was part of their existence. Sure, the children I coached liked to win, but for most of them and the other young people playing organized sports, it wasn't everything. For those who did take things a little too seriously, however, I reminded them that if I ever saw them crying after a game, they'd better be injured. In simpler terms, I was trying to reinforce the notion that they shouldn't place so much stress on themselves that they couldn't afford to lose.

Looking back, being in law enforcement gave me a unique perspective on coaching, and vice versa. The more I reinforced the principles of good sportsmanship with these children – that you mustn't pressure yourself to try to win at any cost; that you must treat your competitors with respect; that tomorrow is another day – the more I found I applied these principles in my work. Yes, I was driven to catch criminals and crack down on gang activity, but if I failed one day to make an important arrest, I knew that I'd have another chance the next day.

Life is full of small and meaningful moments which, if you remain aware, can provide lasting life lessons. I vividly recall a time several years ago when I was going through a particularly tough period at work. Gang rivalries in L.A. were inflamed and gang-related crime was mounting. Despite our best efforts, however, my investigative unit wasn't enjoying much in the way of success. As an experienced member of the team who expected a lot from himself, I felt frustrated and at the early stages of burnout.

I knew I needed an escape from work, so I accepted a unique opportunity to coach a group of inexperienced girls who formed a soccer team at a high school situated in a low-income community. All the girls were Hispanic and only two of them had ever been in an organized game with real uniforms and referees. Since I knew that no one else was interested in spending time with these girls, I elected to take on the role.

I worked with them for about two weeks, focusing on the fundamentals like using both feet to kick the ball and not touching the ball with your hands. Like I said, we're talking basic! Unfortunately, we had a practice game scheduled from the previous year which I debated whether to cancel or not since my girls were just not ready, and our opponents were a team composed of highly skilled club players. Try as I might to be hopeful, I knew the outcome of the game wasn't going to be pretty.

On the day of the practice game, we boarded a school bus and travelled to the school where our opponent was waiting. In contrast to our players, the other team was comprised of upper-middle class, mostly white girls, who were already on field warming up in an organized and efficient manner. They looked somewhat amused when they saw us, perhaps because my girls were more interested in admiring themselves in the uniforms that they wore for the first time, than they were in preparing themselves for the game. Yes, I knew we were going to take a beating, but I considered this game ground zero and the point from which we would mark our improvement for the rest of the season. I was simply going to try to stay positive.

I spent the afternoon offering instructions and encouragement to our overwhelmed group of girls, but when it was all over, we had lost 11-0. During the quiet trip home on the bus, my mind raced with strategies, ideas and sayings I could use in my planned post-game locker room chat to prevent the girls from quitting the team after just one practice game. What would Vince Lombardi of Green Bay Packer fame say at a time like this? What pearls of wisdom could I dredge from my sports' fanatic brain to ease their pain? After all, they lost by a football score and were humiliated by the others. I was their leader, and it was now my task to deliver the words of inspiration that would re-kindle their spirit and make them want to play another day.

We arrived back at our school, exited the bus, and began our long walk toward the locker room for my speech. But before we could get there, one of the girls ran up to me, put her arm around my shoulder and exclaimed, "Coach Tony, when are we gonna play our next game? This was the most fun that we've ever had!"

I was pleasantly surprised, relieved and proud of their maturity. Three weeks later, we played the same team in a tournament and they beat us again, 5-2. The other team had to work hard for that win this time though. After the game, the opposing coaches raved about the progress of our girls, who had gained the respect of a bunch of "rich white girls" who kicked our butts just twenty days earlier. That post-game chat dealt little with soccer, but about the truism that sincere, hard work gains respect....not fear, force and bullets. Happily, we went on to win three games that year, including a win over our arch-rivals.

My experience with these young women sticks with me to this day and reinforces the treasures that may lie in positive pursuits outside of work. The girls and I had gone through the same experience that day when we were pasted 11-0, but the difference was their point of reference and frame of mind. They saw opportunity, while I saw defeat – at least until I learned that the girls had fun. The sheer joy of competing expressed by my team was the medicine that reminded me of the value of staying positive; of the need to not get too wound up about temporary set-backs along the path of life. Just as I think I helped make these kids better athletes and better people, their desire to compete for the fun of it made me a better coach and a better police officer. In short, being a good teacher made me a good student. This lesson was timely, as it snapped me out of my imminent burnout and reinforced the need to be patient when doing challenging police work.

Your escape need not be coaching, of course. It could be solitary activities like writing, reading or running, or it could be group or family activities like camping, travel or volunteer work. It need not be just one thing, either. There could be things you do alone to clear your head that act as a decompression buffer between your work and your family life. And there could be things that you do with your family, as a way of re-establishing connections and intimacy with the people who care about you most. The latter point is particularly important, as you can quickly alienate yourself from the people you love by only pursuing solitary activities. When things at work aren't going so well, you'll come to appreciate the loving support and comfort only your family can provide.

The point is to try to create a mental hideaway, away from your work, that is easily accessible. You don't need two expensive weeks in Tahiti to renew yourself, you just need to periodically recharge by doing something outside work that you enjoy and look forward to. You need a positive, non-destructive, counterbalancing force that satisfies you, stretches your limits and ideally, exemplifies who you are or what you want to become. This means, of course, no drug or alcohol abuse, excessive gambling, or even sitting around with fellow officers after work marking time and griping about how bad your respective situations are. Regrettably, I have witnessed many law enforcement officers fall victim to the temptation of these negative things, all of which made their situations far worse.

Rest assured, there will be times when work stinks and your tolerance for police works plummets to hypoglycemic levels. You may not like your new partner or you may be finding it difficult to acclimate your body to shift work. Your unit may be chronically understaffed or you may be under review for failing to implement a departmental policy correctly. The media might be hounding you for answers as to why gangs are proliferating or you may have been passed over for a specialty assignment. Whatever situation you find yourself in, remember that you're not working twenty-four hours a day, seven days a week. Understand also that you are also not indispensable; you are important, but your police department functions just fine when you are not there. Take a break - and the time - to reward yourself. You'll be glad you did, and better for the experience.

18

Learn From Your Emotional Baptism

You were not born a winner, and you were not born a loser. You are what you make yourself be.

LOU HOLTZ

In law enforcement circles, training is a vital and critical issue. Generally speaking, the better trained your personnel, the more effective they will be. Indeed, even before a candidate enters a police academy, he or she is assessed with respect to how "trainable" they are likely to be.

After entering the academy, the candidate is trained and trained and then trained some more. Candidates are trained on countless law enforcement related subjects, and pass or fail based on how they handle and complete their training. Even after the academy, we receive many hours of in-service training that is designed to reinforce or acquaint us with additional methods of dealing with the issues and problems that may potentially surface. Indeed, our career and livelihood in law enforcement depends on our reaction to, and acceptance of, training.

Much of law enforcement is reactive by nature. When on patrol, we react to radio calls, visual stimuli, information provided by others, and how others deal with us. It's no wonder that a lot of our training has been developed to enable us to react quickly, decisively and appropriately to a given situation. Many times, our reaction determines our effectiveness in dealing with the situation. We encounter and we react. Our training helps us.

Our experience compliments our training. The better you are trained, and the more experience you have, the quicker the reaction. The quicker the reaction, the safer you will be.

One of the subjects to which we are extensively sensitized during formal training is that of the use of deadly force. We are asked whether we can, or will, take another person's life if we have to. We are asked whether we have what it takes to do so, and whether we believe that we will react properly when presented with a situation that may require such a drastic action. We are told that sometimes our reaction to the situation, after the fact, may be unpredictable, and that the impact of our actions will have broad impact on everyone involved.

I took seriously the prospect of this kind of "emotional baptism", and prepared extensively for it alongside my rookie police department counterparts. We were told time and time again that if we visualized a given situation, that we would be better prepared to react to it because we had already "seen it", at least in our mind's eye. Good cops visualize and anticipate things that they've never even encountered, as they want to enhance their ability to react without surprise.

In the preparation for my emotional baptism, I always thought that the hard part would be dealing with the gravity of the situation. After my initial training, I felt pretty squared away as an officer, and believed that if I was involved in a deadly force situation, I wouldn't wing out or react totally out of character. I always knew that if I had to take a life, I would, because that what was sometimes required of a law enforcement officer sworn to ensure public safety. Trying to be a good cop, I'd go over imaginary situations and react to them. I honestly believed I was ready for any emotional trauma that would come my way, including that of firing my weapon into the chest of a criminal intent on doing the same to me. I knew that day may come, so I continually prepared.

Unfortunately, when my time came, I was not as well prepared as I thought I would be.

I had been out of the academy about six months. I was doing well and had been involved in car chases, physical altercations, incidents involving armed suspects, and others situations requiring critical split-second decisions. I was satisfied with my progress as a young probationary officer and felt strongly that I could handle anything that came my way.

Famous NBA coach Pat Riley wrote in his book, *The Winner Within*, of a magic moment in every contest that defines winning from losing. Riley says that every warrior understands this and seizes the moment by giving an effort so intensive and intuitive that it can only be called "one from the heart". It is the warrior stepping up to take on the challenge at the critical point in time.

In my first six months, I thought I had been through some of those defining moments Coach Riley wrote of, and felt increasingly confident with every passing day. I felt good about myself, because I knew that confidence was very important in the make-up of a young officer. Indeed, to this day when I teach recruits at our academy, I tell them that they must absolutely establish self-confidence in their ability, because without it they will hesitate to make a decision when one becomes necessary.

On the evening in question - New Year's Eve - I was still on probation but progressing very well. I had the hang of police work and loved the job, and I was enthused with all aspects of my working life. This was my first New Year's Eve as a police officer and I was working the p.m. watch, roughly 3:00 p.m. to midnight. There were to be no celebrations for me but I knew it came with the job, so no big deal.

My regular training officer was off that day so I was assigned a reserve officer for my shift. Reserve officers are (and were) volunteers from the community who undergo an extensive amount of training (there's that word again) and, upon graduation from the reserve police academy, actually work shifts in the patrol cars with the regular officers. They serve a great purpose, especially with the manpower crunch so many police agencies experience. They are extremely dedicated people who have other jobs and volunteer to work a couple of shifts per month.

The fact that they were assigning a reserve officer to me still a probationary officer - showed that my supervisors had great confidence in my progress and abilities. The fact that it was New Year's Eve made it even more challenging in my mind, as it was a great opportunity for me to prove to myself that I could handle the unique circumstances that often arose on such a night.

The reserve officer was very attentive and a real good guy. We had an uneventful shift except for the last call of the night. The radio call we received was for a "death investigation" at a local emergency hospital. There was no tone of urgency connected to the call. Many times in the case of a natural death, the police are dispatched to make sure there are no signs of foul play. The great majority of these types of radio calls normally involve elderly people who are in poor health and succumb to their ailment.

Since I was relatively new on the job, I knew that if there were any doubts surrounding the circumstances of any death, I could summon an on-call detective from the department's Detective Headquarters Division and he would respond and make any critical decisions. As we drove to the hospital, I anticipated that this was going to end as a quiet, uneventful night…but I was wrong.

When we arrived at the emergency ward of the hospital, we encountered a man and a woman in their forties, both crying, along with a teen aged girl who was also visibly upset. The woman was especially distraught and emotional, not an unusual reaction in the death of a loved one. The Fire Department ambulance was also at the hospital in the emergency ward and one of the paramedics came over to brief me, the officer in charge, on the circumstances surrounding the death.

What I learned was that the deceased was a three-month old infant, a tiny little girl. The young baby died in her sleep, the apparent victim of Sudden Infant Death Syndrome (SIDS). The dead baby's mother was not around, and was not yet aware of the death of her child, as the baby was being cared for at the time by a 14-year old babysitter who lived next door. Of course, the people we first observed crying were the parents of the babysitter and the babysitter herself. The young babysitter was totally devastated and feeling responsible, and also distressed because the mother of the baby was not aware of what had happened. As we learned, the mother of the baby went out to celebrate New Year's Eve and was to return around 1:00 a.m. She was also supposed to call periodically to check in on her baby, something she hadn't done all evening.

One of the first things that happened at the hospital was that my partner and I were led over to the dead baby's cubicle to see the body. The first staggering, Muhammed Ali-like uppercut I accepted to my head was the sight of a dead baby, for the first time in my life. Other than the fact that she was an unusual color, the baby appeared to be almost doll-like in appearance, particularly since she was not moving or breathing. The nurse who accompanied us moved the baby around in order to show us that there were no signs of trauma or foul play. Then the nurse said, "You can check for yourself."

The second Ali-like punch in the head, this time a right cross, was touching the dead baby. The baby was cold and stiff, and she did not react to my touch. This struck me as very odd because I was already the father of two small kids, my youngest, a daughter, barely a year old. My daughter always reacted to my touch. Whether I was changing her or just playing with her, she always moved back.

The dead baby's tiny body also felt very cold. My fatherly instinct was to pick her up and try to warm her in my arms. I caught myself and left the baby cold and alone on the hospital gurney. There was nothing I could do for that poor baby; I was powerful, yet powerless in the moment. A very deep sadness set in on me, unlike any I had experienced as a young cop or a young man. It mattered none that I was conditioned and trained to be strong and stay in control, even in the midst of tragedy and turmoil. But this was different. I couldn't even warm the cold, motionless baby in my arms. What kind of father was I? What kind of cop?

To that point in my career, when there were a lot of things going on at a radio call or situation, I was able to watch more seasoned officers handle things and therefore learn from their actions. Now I was in charge, and had to interview the babysitter and the parents. But wait a minute, where was the mom?

I interviewed the babysitter, and later the parents. The babysitter was totally distraught and devastated, feeling guilty because the baby died under her care. She was barely able to speak, but after much consoling on my part, did muster the courage to compose herself just long enough to explain the circumstances surrounding the tragic incident.

I learned that during the evening the babysitter checked on the sleeping baby, and discovered that she wasn't moving. Upon closer inspection, the baby appeared to be purple and not breathing. The young babysitter summoned her parents who were in their apartment next door. When the parents encountered the infant, they immediately began to administer CPR and called for an ambulance. The parents of the babysitter could not revive the baby and the paramedics continued their futile attempt to resurrect the young life as they transported her to the emergency department of the closest hospital. When the baby was declared dead at the hospital, the police were notified.

The babysitter was simply a basketcase, no matter how much I tried to comfort her and explain that this was not her fault but simply an extremely tragic incident. Unfortunately, her private hell was only going to get worse. And so was mine.

Not only did I have to deal with the circumstances of this case, I now had to do so alone, as my volunteer reserve partner had to leave. Normally, regular officers stick out their shift, not leaving their partner behind to finish all the work. In the case of a reserve officer, however, they aren't paid so they really can't be expected to stick around on an overtime basis. In this case, there really wasn't any actual work to do, only notifications and maybe some interviews. There was nothing I couldn't do by myself, so I encouraged him to leave and thanked him for the help.

Now on my own, I began to organize the situation in my mind after hearing the account from the babysitter and her parents. I had a dead three-month old baby who was being watched by a 14-year old girl. The baby died in her sleep. The babysitter had done nothing wrong, but now felt responsible for the baby's death. She was devastated and barely able to talk. Her parents were visibly shaken because they didn't know what to expect, much less how to comfort their daughter. The deceased baby's mother went out to party on New Year's Eve, left the baby with the young babysitter and hadn't been heard from since. She didn't even know her baby was dead. And there was no father in the picture.

As I continued to organize my thoughts, I was pleased to learn that I would receive some support from detective headquarters, who were dispatching a detective to handle the investigation at the scene of the baby's death - the home. That was one less thing for me to worry about in case this whole thing took a turn for the worse and we actually had a crime scene.

I was able to make some positive headway by assuring the parents that their daughter was not at fault and that there wouldn't be any legal ramifications regarding her actions involving the baby's death. Looking back, I really didn't know that at the time, but it's what I believed after speaking to the paramedics. I was able to reassure the parents so that they could concentrate on comforting their daughter. It was a small moral victory for me and afforded me a bit of strength. I would have taken anything positive at that point.

Still no mother…

I had the babysitter and her parents stick around just in case the detective from downtown had any questions. I used some common sense and guessed right on that one just in case there was any foul play, although I still didn't believe it existed.

Where was the mother? My sorrow and grief for the poor mother was now turning to anger and confusion on my part. Where in the hell was she?

Soon thereafter, a patrol supervisor showed up to make sure that everything was under control and that I didn't need anything. He also told me that due to the heavy New Year's Eve call load, I would have to stick around and notify the mother whenever she decided to show up. The patrol supervisor left the hospital satisfied with how the incident was being handled. "Sure Sarge, I'm doing just great…".

Time continued to pass, and still no mother.

About an hour after the sergeant left the hospital, the detective from headquarters showed up. He introduced himself, shook my hand, explained that he was returning from the baby's apartment, and then asked where the involved persons were. I explained to him that the babysitter and her parents were in the lobby waiting for his arrival. He told me that in a normal homicide investigation, I should have separated the involved person from the witnesses so that they couldn't compare notes and get their stories straight.

I snapped at him, "Is this a homicide!?", finally showing signs of my frustration.

The detective calmly replied, "Easy, kid. I'm just giving you something to think about in the future."

I thought to myself, "The future? Evidently the present is doing a great job of kicking my ass. In the future …?"

Then the detective asked me, "Where's the mom?"

Still no mom…

The detective then said we should now inspect the "body" before speaking to the babysitter and her parents. My temperature started to rise and my internal dialogue continued: "Body?...you dumb ass, that wasn't a body, it's a baby". For whatever reason, his referring to the baby as a "body" pissed me off and struck me as insensitive, and I was barely able to conceal my emotions.

We entered the cubicle where the baby rested. The detective uncovered her and began to inspect her body. He didn't do it as a father would check his daughter for an injury. He did it clinically as a professional police officer should, to inspect for possible foul play. The baby deserved that level of attention and the detective was proficient at his work, but he didn't treat the lifeless body gently, and that somehow disturbed me. He then put her down, took some notes and covered her body with a blanket. He also sensed something going on inside me because he looked at me and said, "there's nothing you can do."

Still no mother….

The detective confided in me that he believed that the death was neither a homicide nor due to negligence on anyone's part. Despite this, he was still going to interview everyone as part of the investigation.

The detective skilfully and professionally conducted those interviews under extremely tragic conditions. Maybe it was the fact that he was a detective, or that he was older and more experienced, or that he was wearing a suit and not a uniform, but whatever the reason, he seemed to have a calming affect on the family in the lobby. He instructed them to leave but not go home because he didn't want them to notify the mom when she showed up. That was our job. When he was out at the apartment, the detective had secured the home and left a note on the front door instructing the mom to proceed to the hospital when she arrived at her apartment.

The babysitter and her parents sadly left the hospital, likely emotionally scarred forever. The detective then informed me that he would handle all of the reports. My only responsibility was to wait for the mother to show up at the hospital and notify her of her baby's death. The detective shook my hand, said I did a good job, and left.

Now I had to sit and wait for the mother. Under those conditions, there probably wasn't a better place for a young cop to be than at an emergency hospital. Doctors and nurses are generally very good to cops. There exists a bond between cops and emergency medical personnel because in our own separate way, we have to deal with many of the same traumatic things that life thrusts upon us. Our heads, collectively, are in the mouth of the dragon.

Periodically, a nurse or other staff member would ask if I needed anything. They could see, though, that I wanted to be alone with my emotions, and for the most part, they let me be.

Hours passed and still no mom. Emotionally, I was on one hell of a roller coaster. I would think of the poor, cold baby and feel like crying. I would then think of the poor babysitter and her now tarnished life. I hoped that her parents would grow stronger, for their daughter's sake. Then I would think of that stupid ass mother who didn't seem to care much about her baby daughter and who was probably still partying somewhere, oblivious to the fact that her daughter was now stone-cold dead.

I would think about my own children and how they touched back when I touched them. I would think of how lucky I was to have them, and how badly I wanted to hold them at that moment in time.

I also wondered why I was going through all of these emotions, why this situation affected me so profoundly despite all the training I had received. Self doubt began to creep into my psyche, and I began to wonder if I really had what it took to be a cop. Good cops don't let things get to them. At least that is what they told me in the academy.

For hours and hours, I shuffled these emotions inside of me like a black jack dealer handles cards in a Las Vegas casino. Still no mom. Shuffle…shuffle…shuffle. "OK anger, rotate; bring on sorrow" I thought to myself.

I was also getting ready and building myself up for inevitable confrontation with the mother. About 7:30 a.m., two patrol officers showed up at the hospital. They told me that I was relieved and that they would take over from my post and therefore notify the mom. Since I had made a considerable time and emotional investment in this case over the previous ten hours or so, I resisted their offer, but really had no choice but to depart. As suddenly as that, my role was over. I went home.

On the way home, I continued to run through my mix of emotions and added another – frustration. I had wanted to face the mom, and give her a piece of my mind. But my emotions seemed out of place. There were no guns involved, no violent fire-fight with a suspected criminal, no dead body, save for the innocent little infant. Did I really have what it took to be an effective cop?

I got home, kissed and hugged my children and felt great guilt because they were not cold or unable to touch and respond to me. I got my four hours of mid-day sleep and went back to work. When I got there, I felt numb. At my locker, I put on my uniform, badge and gun, and almost magically felt energized.

The uniform, badge and gun didn't protect me from my raw emotions during the long night before, but they did now.

What I learned from that experience is that the gravity of a given situation is not what psychologically or emotionally catches us off guard, thereby making our reactions unpredictable, like when we use deadly force against someone. Rather, it is the mixture of our emotions, and the management of them, that makes us pass or fail, quit or go on, fight or run away.

I had juggled countless emotions the previous night, but had resolved them and therefore was ready for more police work. It took a little time, and a lot of pain, but it produced a great spiritual victory for me, a step forward in my maturation process. It meant I could go on, even after being a little wounded. It meant I was resilient and committed, and that I would be a good cop after all.

There is no substitute for being well-trained and prepared to react properly on a moment's notice. But there will be times when you'll have to stop and think about what you are doing and feeling, because your hundreds of hours of previous training are incapable of invoking an automatic response. The need to think our way out of a challenge is what defines us as humans, and as cops. Perhaps these are the moments Coach Riley referred to, the ones that require a "one from the heart" effort so intensive and intuitive, that they serve to differentiate the winners from the losers.

It's okay for us cops and first responders to have feelings. The difficult times are when multiple feelings betray us and race in opposite directions. It's going to happen. What's most important is how you handle your feelings. So, don't punish yourself for being vulnerable or letting something touch you deep inside. It's just a sign that you are human. And from my vast experience, I can tell you that humans still make the best cops.

19

You Can't Change People, But You Can Influence Them

Change your thoughts and you change your world.

NORMAN VINCENT PEALE

In the past twenty-plus years, I have been blessed with the opportunity to travel and conduct training throughout North America for law enforcement personnel, educators, parents, corrections officials and other professionals. Consistently, regardless of where I am, and the nature, size and severity of their gang problem, certain factors and trends regarding youth and gang membership emerge.

The gang problem is not a Los Angeles, Chicago, Toronto or other big city problem. It is not a minority problem. It is not even an immigration or economic disparity problem. The gang problem is a people problem, and it affects all segments of our society.

I have never really thought of the gang problem as a juvenile delinquency issue, because most of the gang members with whom I have dealt were actually young adults. It is true, however, that at the time the decision is made by an individual to join a gang, he or she is normally under the age of 18. In Los Angeles, because of the tradition of third and fourth generation gang members, the majority of gang members are adults. They were juveniles who, for whatever reason, continued their gang behavior well into adulthood. I do realize that in many emerging gang cities, however, gangs are predominantly a juvenile delinquency matter.

I have come in contact with a great many hard working and dedicated front line professionals, both those in and outside law enforcement. These devoted and self-sacrificing individuals have one common mission: to save young people. In the good old days, that was the primary responsibility of the child's parents. Unfortunately, these aren't the good old days any longer.

Without proper leadership and support in the home, the child goes elsewhere. Gangs provide an alternative to the conventional family. With the breakdown of the family structure as we know it, more and more kids are joining gangs. They are also dropping out of school, using drugs and alcohol, getting pregnant and doing all of the things that lead kids down the wrong path in life.

Nowadays, professionals like us have more responsibility for what happens to young people, even if they are not our own kids. Cops, educators, counselors, probation officers, school administrators and community leaders all have to take part in saving young people from the streets. The big problem for us is that we don't always know if we're doing a good job, or even making a difference at all. Sometimes, when we look at the continued growth of the gang problem, our efforts may seem futile.

One of the things I have learned along the way is that the war to keep kids out of gangs is a hard fought one with many fronts. No simple and quick fix solution exists that will put an end to this war, either. In other words, there exists no metaphorical nuclear bomb which, when used, renders the enemy incapable of fighting again.

This is a war of foot soldiers. On society's side, the foot soldiers are the committed street cops, teachers and front line professionals who deal with all manner of people. They are the ones who regularly see the hurt, anguish and disappointment only life, and street gangs, can provide. On the other side of the battle line are the gangs, drugs, abusive and neglectful parents, and negative influences that make it easy for our kids to give up and give in. As professionals who have enlisted for this war, we know that no one person has the answer or secret formula for a problem that has taken decades to form; we know that this war will take years to win.

Normally, the young people who join gangs are not very happy with their station in life. They are not satisfied with the amount of love, support and attention they receive, nor are they comfortable with their identity, lack of success or the generally low expectations placed upon them. In their minds, gangs can resolve many of these troubling issues and provide, often for the first time, a unified sense of belonging, if not "family". Despite all of the negative connotations and ramifications associated with gangs, kids still join them because they are deriving some benefits.

I have always believed that as an active participant in the fight against violent gangs, part of my mission is to use my power and position to influence youth in a positive way whenever possible. When young people are around, adults have important responsibilities because youth watch, listen and learn. When young people are watching and listening to me, I've always tried to make them think. Young people who are thinking about joining a gang, abusing drugs or dropping out of school must be made to think about the possible consequences. They must be made to question their own behavior and the negative influences around them, instead of merely accepting them.

One of the best ways to make them question their behavior or the gang life itself is to point out the many contradictions. As a case in point, my partner and I were driving down the street in Newton Street Division one evening a few years back when we came upon a group of kids in the middle of the street on their bicycles. There were about 6 or 7 of them, a group composed of both blacks and Hispanics. On a typical good day, I would pull up and chit-chat with anyone, just trying to remain approachable and familiar in the neighborhood. We stopped our car and the children, aged between 9 and 12 years, immediately gathered around my yellow Plymouth Fury. One of them then deadpanned, "Hey Pacman, the guys who hang on that corner say you're a little punk." He was obviously trying to get a reaction out of me.

In an exaggerated and overblown manner, I sat up and looked back at the corner and said loudly, "Who said that?" They got a real kick out of my response and were all laughing at the way I was clowning around with them. I knew from the young person's question that he was referring to the local Crip gang that would hang around in the parking lot adjacent to a busy business street.

Continuing with my act, I then moved to serious mode by lowering my voice and motioning to all the kids to move in closer, as if I were about to tell them a big secret. I then said to them, "If my partner and I leave and come back later and those guys are in the lot drinking and smoking, and we come around the corner real fast and slam on the brakes, what do you think they'll do?"

The leader of the pack said, "Run like hell". The other youth were in unanimous agreement with him.

I then asked, "Why would they run?"

"Because you're the police and you got guns," was the reply.

Then I said, "OK. We're sitting here talking to you guys and we can sit here all night. What happens if a carload of gangsters, all with guns, comes around the corner in a car real fast and they slam on the brakes while we're here. Do you think we're going to run?"

The answer from the group was "no way!"

With a big grin, I sat up proudly and said, "Well then, who's the little punk?"

That stopped them in their tracks. They all looked at each other and nodded in agreement. One of them said, "They're the little punks!"

I smiled and said, "Yep … I'm not running from anyone." The kids then all smiled and rode off, waving goodbye to me and my partner.

I would see the spokesman for that group from time to time in the neighborhood. As he got older, I noticed that he started to get that hardened look. I would pop my head out the car window and yell, "Remember who the little punk is!"

I never saw him get into trouble and don't believe he ever joined the local gang, but years later he told me that he remembered that little talk with him and the boys. He said that he remembered how much sense that made to him. That made me feel pretty good, and reinforced my belief that we made a difference.

I don't know what ever happened to him. I did my part that evening in South-Central Los Angeles to try to convince him and his "boys" that gangsters, and not cops and law abiding citizens, were the real punks. Looking back, the interesting thing about this example was the relative simplicity of the moment. I managed to reach these boys during a casual encounter on the street. Unlike primetime television, there were no dramatic events that led to their "deathbed conversion" insofar as their attitudes on gangs were concerned. Rather, it was a small turn of the wheel that helped them navigate safely through some of Los Angeles' toughest streets. You see, the thing about this war is that victory requires a thousand little moves and a thousand little victories; victory never comes all at once. Think about all the little decisions you've made in your life - was their one decision that in retrospect initially appeared small but turned out to be life changing? If enough of our foot soldiers remain committed enough to reach young people and make them think, then it might be just enough to make a difference between a life of despair versus a life of success.

It is important, however, to take the long view on this matter and not get discouraged. For example, I was once approached by a much respected school administrator who had just seen a video of a prison riot as part of a training session at a gang conference. She was a bit bewildered by the video and asked me how she could possibly believe that she was doing an adequate job after witnessing the taped riot. She was responsible for administering the discipline at a high school and prided herself in taking extra time with each kid to resolve their issues. She cared deeply about the welfare of young people, but wondered if educators, police and others were simply losing the fight. She said to me, "How could there be violent prison riots if all of us are doing our jobs right?"

My reply to her was "You can't determine your effectiveness by watching a video of a prison riot. If you weren't around and doing your job, there may have been 125 inmates involved in that riot instead of 100. Maybe 5 would have been killed rather than just the one that was killed. Your accomplishments lie in the youth who weren't caught up in that riot because they weren't in prison in the first place."

As a society, we are accustomed to immediate feedback and quick gratification. The problem, however, is that we don't see immediate results from our efforts to help kids stay on the right path. As foot soldiers, we just have to do our job to the best of our abilities and trust that our allies on the next beachhead or in the next village are doing their jobs and are committed to the same course. Perhaps as important as just trying to make a kid think, then, is maintaining your sense of calm and a healthy dose of patience as you fight the good fight.

I never believed, and still don't believe, that I could turn around a hard core gang member who is committed to the life-style and enjoys gangbanging. Neither do I believe that serving time in prison is going to make any difference to a person who has little interest in living a more balanced and wholesome life. For the baddest of the bad who like being gangsters, little we can say, or do, will change their ways.

The best that cops and corrections officials can do when dealing with those at risk of joining a gang or those who are gang involved but who have not progressed to the status of "hard-core", is to make them think. And if you can make them think, you may just influence them for the better.

20

Develop Your Own Style of Working Gangs

A sense of humor is part of the art of leadership, of getting along with people, of getting things done.

DWIGHT D. EISENHOWER

When I initially became interested in working gangs back in the 70s, there existed no strategy manual or playbook that instructed a young officer how to do this kind of police work and what kind of style to employ to produce the biggest returns.

Back then, your option was to learn from veteran officers by watching how they dealt with gang members on the street. The problem was, however, that many experienced officers weren't very creative about working gangs, largely because of the hatred that existed between cops and gang members. The average cop would deal with gang members straight on, in a by-the-book, enforce the law to-the-max kind of way. While I understood the often violent circumstances that gave rise to the deep and long resentment between law enforcement officers and gang members, I felt that there was something more that could be done than simply write gangsters tickets, make some arrests, lock them up or bust heads.

Intuitively, I knew that to be effective in my chosen profession, I needed to get to know gang members and their way of life. The seasoned officers I respected were, in my mind, better than the rest because they were committed to getting to know things. I thought that it didn't take an exceptionally talented cop to drive around all day answering radio calls, writing tickets or making an arrest here and there. Doing the grunt work of policing was important, I knew that. But I wanted more; I wanted to Be like the officers I admired who made it their business to be in the know and therefore were capable of operating at a higher level of performance.

While television programs and movies suggested otherwise, I knew that a scruffy and streetwise undercover cop couldn't just show up in a neighborhood, act cool and be initiated into the gang, where he would then covertly conduct his important police work. In the normal gang culture and tradition back then, gang members were usually born and raised in the neighborhoods they represented. People had deep ties and multi-generational connections within their community, which precluded any chance of infiltration by a new cop. This may - and I stress may - be easier now. People are more mobile and transient, and generally have less attachment to their communities than they did twenty and thirty years ago. Relationships run deep though, and this still makes it difficult for an outsider to obtain an insider's view of the gang by process of infiltration.

Fresh out of police academy, there's no way I could have infiltrated the "Barrio Van Nuys" gang in Van Nuys Division where I was initially deployed on patrol. Even though I was Mexican-American, understood the Hispanic gang culture, spoke the language and could easily play the part since I grew up around gang members, there was absolutely no way I would have been trusted in that neighborhood. Someone would have to "co-sign" for me. If an outside gang member moved into that neighborhood and wanted to hang with the local guys, they would first verify his background from someone in their old neighborhood. In the gang world, everyone knows someone from somewhere else. Ironically, the correctional system promotes that network because gangsters from rival gangs and neighborhoods are forced to actually live together while in custody. Again, there existed no *Gang Work for Dummies* book, so I had to figure out a way to get to know gang members and their environment. I had to create my own method. I had to develop my own style.

I knew that gangsters didn't like cops. If I waited on a street corner for them to approach me, I would still be standing at that very spot, 28 years later! Since they wouldn't come to me, I had to go to them. If they were to be my primary instructors, I had to make the initial contact. To me, it was like the sport of fishing. I could read extensively about fishing and learn about the latest and most effective equipment, lures and casting techniques. But in order to actually *catch* fish, I had to go to the pond and drop a line in the water. Initiating contact with gang members was the equivalent of dropping my line in the water.

In a police division where there was in excess of 30 street gangs, I knew I could become overwhelmed, chase my tail and never accomplish much if I elected to "go to school" with all of them. I decided to learn one gang first, and they would be the test case upon which I would establish and build my expertise. This early decision, I believe, was the first indication or emergence of my style – to go slow, be committed, and learn to walk before I could run with respect to any gang.

I therefore set a goal to be the most knowledgeable person on a particular gang in my police division. Initially, I learned the basics that were readily available but that few of my peers actually bothered to learn, such as their name, abbreviations, symbols, graffiti, ethnicity, boundaries, rivals, allies, tendencies and criminal activity. I quickly came to realize that the more a police officer knew about a specific gang and gangs in general, the more gang members would talk to them and the less they would lie. In keeping with my style to observe and learn, I watched carefully how other officers interacted with gang members. Whether it was a traffic stop, radio call, field interview or arrest situation, I saw that gang members just didn't volunteer information. I experienced this first hand several times as a rookie. When asked a question that they believed they could get away with, the gang member would lie or just clam up completely.

If you think of a gang as a secret society, its members will not simply volunteer information to the average Joe on the street. That information is definitely not offered to law enforcement and to do so is a sign of weakness on the part of the member who talks. Now, if you have a secret and I approach you and discuss the secret openly, the cat is out of the bag and for you to talk about it isn't such a big deal anymore. Knowledge is power, and my inherent style dictated that doing my homework was, above all else, the key to being effective in my profession and indeed the most valuable use of my time.

With respect to contacting gang members, most officers thought in terms of "probable cause" or "lawful detention" (today, we can add the ever-controversial term "profiling" to this lexicon). These phrases were, and will always be, front and center in an officer's mind when the decision is made to interact with a gang member. These considerations are very important and I respect them to this day, but there is nothing inappropriate about a police officer talking, laughing and conversing with members of their community, even those who are gang members.

If I was standing in line in uniform at a fast food restaurant waiting to order and a woman and her child engaged me in conversation, I would naturally oblige. To not do so would have been inappropriate and discourteous on my part. Take the same situation and replace the woman and child with a gang member. I felt it was perfectly appropriate and lawful to engage in a conversation with that person, regardless of the fact that he may have led a less than respectable life.

Initially, I would offer the gang member the same courtesy and respect I would offer any citizen. To do less would be wrong. That also meant I could ask questions like "How are things going?" or "Is everything quiet?" The majority of the time, the response was positive. They might not have given me the key to the secret information vault, but they would talk nonetheless, usually because it was not an official contact and no one was being searched or handcuffed. They didn't feel the tension that normally existed between cops and gangsters on the street.

As a strategy, I knew that the ability to converse confidently with gang members and to draw information from them was essential, but I discovered that its effectiveness depended almost entirely on one's style. Take the previous fast food example. People are naturally curious about police officers and their work.

Many times, whether people actually say anything to you or not is determined by your overall look, body language and demeanor. If you hide your eyes behind mirrored sunglasses, never crack a smile, adopt an aggressive stance and never initiate contact, you may be perceived as aloof or unapproachable, the tough and unrelenting cop that people love to hate. But if you remain friendly, open and approachable, people will engage you in conversation, sometimes providing you with key intelligence to help you do your job better.

Same thing with gang members, I quickly learned. As I've said, my personality was that of a gregarious, fun-loving, Don Rickles impersonator when it came time to deal with gang members. When I was on patrol in the neighborhood of a particular gang I was studying, I would take the opportunity to stop and talk to the local gang members, much as I would with the other citizens who lived there. My style was relaxed, calm and professional, and I would try to make people laugh in a gregarious, but not buffoon kind of way. As a result, people opened up and began to trust me.

When I stopped gang members within the legal guidelines of probable cause, I engaged them in relaxed banter, yet interviewed them in a matter-of-fact fashion that ensured, among other things, that I learned their respective nicknames or monikers. Since my style was perceived as relaxed and not overly-confrontational, gang members shared this crucial information, which really represented the gang member's street identity or "calling card". Knowing that one gang member was "Psycho" and the other "Lucky" gave me a unique view of the gang and its internal dynamics.

Once I learned them, I would refer to each gang member by their moniker. This achieved a couple things. First, it let them know that I indeed knew who they were, which immediately distinguished me from the vast majority of others cops who patrolled their streets. I cannot tell you strongly enough the inherent power in being able to stop five gangsters, and rhyme off their monikers one by one. It showed them that I was sharp and knew my stuff, and they talked to me more and lied to me less as a result. Second, as I would encounter more and more gang members, the ones I didn't know would, on their own volition, offer me up their moniker just because I knew everyone else's. It was if they felt left out because I could refer to their fellow gangsters by their street handle, but not by theirs!

It was in this way that I developed, and imposed, my personality and style on gang members. If gang members were in a public parking lot congregating, I would stop and talk to them. When you have gang members congregating, it creates an optimum target for rivals to do a drive-by shooting or mount an attack. In a public place, this puts everyone in the general area in jeopardy and can create a safety hazard. If, during my chit-chat with the gangsters someone got offended and claimed that they weren't bothering anyone, I would just explain that I was being sociable and making sure that all was safe. In all the years I've suggested I was there to ensure their safety, I've never once had a gang member argue with my logic, other than to say that they could take care of themselves.

If gang members were in the front yard of a residence or in an apartment building, I would stop and talk. Sometimes I would get out of the car, sometimes I wouldn't. In one neighborhood I was patrolling it was not uncommon for me to stop and talk to anyone, even "normal people". I was nosey, yes, but all the while conducted myself in a friendly and cordial way. I was also gaining respect and picking up scraps of information here and there.

In the rare times I was a hard ass or all business, I got stonewalled and avoided. In contrast, when I was a happy-go-lucky neighborhood cop, I was accepted and tolerated as part of the landscape. I found that my style really worked, and I gathered a more valuable dimension of knowledge when I worked my gang beat in this way. Yes, substance was important, but so was an amenable personal style that was conducive to extracting actionable information. After I developed and refined my style of learning a neighborhood, working a gang and being familiar to members of that community, I was able to apply it to any gang. My only real limitation was time – you can have the will and the ability, but sometimes not enough time.

Unfortunately, one's cordiality and openness to gang members can be misinterpreted by some people in your community, but that still is a small price to pay in relation to the benefits of the approach. Years ago, a captain informed me that a citizen had called his office and complained that I was always talking and joking around with gang members, but never took them to jail "where they belonged", as the concerned citizen put it. The captain explained to the upset caller that I was doing what I was paid to do - get to know gang members - and that no one could be arrested before they committed a crime.

For me, my style was a natural extension of my open, jovial and inquisitive personality, and it was effective in getting my foot in the door as far as a particular gang was concerned. While the fundamentals of my style have almost universal application as far as working gangs are concerned (e.g., study a gang, learn monikers, be approachable, ask questions, study some more), the way I expressed myself may not work for everyone.

The key is to employ a style that is natural for you, one with which you are comfortable and one you can rely upon in the most challenging of circumstances. If you craft a style that is contrived, people may recognize it as such and you'll be considered manipulative or untrustworthy. So, if you are like me and naturally have a happy and inquisitive disposition, try that style and see how it works. If you are more serious or reserved by nature, you can still employ that style so long as you remain approachable and amenable in the field. And if your natural style is akin to Sheriff Buford T. Justice of *Smokey and the Bandit* fame, well, develop a new one, fast!

Watch other officers and professionals and see what is effective for them. Think about what you could do to improve what you see and note what might work for you. Since developing an effective policing style is more art than science, you must use your life experiences, common sense, instinct and trial and error, to craft a style that will serve you well and keep you safe. There is no right, off-the-shelf style that you can use; it's about learning when to use strength, and learning when to use finesse; it's about investing the time and attention to develop your own unique style.

I once had a captain put out a directive to all patrol officers in our division that if an officer was seen talking to a gang member, he'd better be taking him to jail. That captain never worked gangs, he never had his own style, and he never understood how it could be a very effective law enforcement tool.

21

Acres of Diamonds In Your Backyard

Women must not depend upon the protection of man, but must be taught to protect themselves..

SUSAN B. ANTHONY

Gangs are a male dominated world. Gangs were first designed by males for males. Nowadays, gangs in the Southern California area are comprised of over 90% male members, and I would imagine that this ratio is consistent throughout North America.

Males normally decide the gang name, establish the boundaries, determine the gang's allies and enemies and make most of the major decisions pertaining to the gang. When you do find female gang members, they are normally a small part of the traditional male gang, rather than part of a distinct female gang. In my part of California, we don't encounter the "Daisy-Mae's" or the "Versace Girls" feuding with the 18th Street Gang over turf and drug markets. I have encountered female cliques or subsets of a traditional gang, but never a female gang. If female gangs exist in Los Angeles, they are flying way under the radar and have no impact on the overall gang picture.

The female gang member has a lesser role in the gang than the normal male member. The females are involved in criminal activity, but many times they are committing different types of crimes. In general terms, the males are pulling the trigger, doing the stabbing, trafficking the drugs and calling the shots. The females, in contrast, are normally into prostitution, theft, fraud and property crimes, smuggling and concealing contraband and gathering intelligence for the gang.

Many of the females I have known to be influential within a gang weren't actual members. For example, some females have influence in a gang because their boyfriend or husband is a gang leader in custody and the female is the conduit through which the gang member continues to participate in or run the gang. Therefore, while she is not an actual gang member, she nonetheless represents a significant player as she sees to it that the gang leader's orders are carried out.

In 1998, I conducted an audit of violent gang crimes that occurred in the city of Los Angeles. I found that over 6,700 murders, attempted murders and felony assaults were deemed gang related. Only 1% of those 6,700 crimes were committed by female gang members. My audit also indicated that non-gang member females accounted for almost one-quarter of the victims of these violent crimes. Many of these girls were associates of actual gang members that got caught up in a gang attack.

While many researchers, gang specialists and academics insist that female gang members are just as deadly as their male counterparts and are getting worse, I don't believe that female gang members are nearly as violent as the males and think that statistics would support this notion. This is not to suggest that we should let down our guard when dealing with female gang members. However, we need to keep a proper perspective on the scope and qualities of the female gang member issue, otherwise we may mask the greater threat relating to females and gangs, that being the impact that gangs have on females as a gender.

Assume for a moment that there is a gang comprised of 100 members in your community. There are 90 male members, and there are 10 female members. Now, the gang world is a heterosexual, macho and territorial world where strength, intimidation and image are tools of the trade. So in our example, let's assume that the 10 female gang members have love interests or boyfriends in the gang itself, which therefore leaves 80 male gang members without females for their girlfriends, love interests and wives. Where do you think those 80 gang members will go for their women? Let's face it; they troll for females in your community. They get their girlfriends from your neighborhood, your friends, your associates....and even from your own family. You get the picture?

I have talked with countless parents across the country, including those working in law enforcement, and have heard many heartbreaking stories about daughters who got caught up in the gang mix. While the specific circumstances surrounding these stories vary, imagine this typical scenario.

Let's say you have a 15-year old daughter who is a straight "A" student, an all-star soccer player, regularly attends church with your family and helps take care of her younger siblings. She is a delight to have as a daughter and you are proud of who she has grown to become and where she is going. Then, your nice young lady falls in love with a gang member. You will now have a whole world of problems with your child.

Her attitude will change for the worse. Her interests will shift, and so will the way she dresses. Her grades will eventually suffer. She will have a different set of friends. Her priorities will change. She will be secretive about her business. She may begin to abuse drugs or alcohol and engage in risky sexual practices. She will not want to spend time with the family. The worst thing of all is that if she loves this gangster, he can do no wrong in her eyes. She will defend him and his ways. She will wind up doing things she never envisioned, all in the name of what she thinks is love. She will also be in danger because she is socializing in public with a target of other gangs' members and the police.

Love is indeed a powerful thing. We have all heard accounts of good girls who have fallen in love with bad boys. James Dean, at his peak as a movie star outlaw, was adored by women. Highly visible and violent murderers on death row, with no possible prospect of living in civil society ever again, get love letters and marriage propositions from women whom they have never met. Organized crime group members always seem to have attractive women close by. Maybe it is the sense of excitement that comes from the unknown, with being involved with someone who lives outside of society's norms, that attract some young people to their polar opposites. While my example above was of a 15-year old girl who fell in love with a gangster and allowed his lifestyle to dictate and ruin her life, a 40-year old woman (your sister, your girlfriend, your wife) could just as easily do the same thing. Our society has come to the point where we can joke about and accept the old saying, "women love outlaws". Because of gangs, however, women love outlaws a lot earlier.

An ex-female gang member with whom I spoke at a training session illustrates well the impact of love with a gangster. "Gangs use girls. It took me a few years before I got the message. I sat in jail for a few months just for holding my guy's drugs. I went to jail for him. The only visits I got were from my mom and my daughter. When the holidays came and left and still I got no other visits, that was it for me. As long as I had a place for him to stay, food for him to eat, money for him to spend, a body for him to enjoy, I was accepted. I was used, like all other girls in that spot."

My unit was once looking for a gang member wanted for murder. We received information suggesting that he was still in contact with his girlfriend. We monitored the girlfriend's activities for a few days to see if she met with him. Not a gang member, the girlfriend was a very attractive Hispanic girl with a good job and a nice family background. We learned that her family hated the gangster boyfriend because they knew what he was all about. He was involved in bad things and their daughter was drawn into it, despite their many cautions. Unfortunately, the daughter grew to be more loyal to the gangster than to her own loving family.

The gang member was eventually caught in another state. If she had met up with her boyfriend during our surveillance, she probably would have been arrested for harboring a fugitive. All the while, we felt that she knew his whereabouts, so we really had a case of a good girl helping to hide a murderer. During my unit's debriefing, we discussed the girlfriend. I thought that if we were able to remove her from the situation and have her see herself as we saw her, as her family saw her, she'd probably be surprised and ask herself. "How did things get so out of hand? How did I get this far? What was I thinking?"

As front-line professionals involved in the ever-present battle with the gang problem, we tend to focus our prevention efforts on youth who are at risk of becoming involved in a gang. Since boys and young men are the primary raw ingredient to the making or growing of a gang, we focus our attention on them. We seek them out and reach from afar to change the way they perceive the world of gangs, because we believe that maybe, just maybe, we can steer them clear of the gang world. But when doing so, we sometimes fail to protect other vulnerable parts of our society - the girls and young women who are closest to us – those who we could never imagine would get sucked into the world of gangs.

Acres of Diamonds is a famous lecture that Russell H. Conwell, the founder of Temple University, delivered thousands of times throughout the United States. It is a fable that tells the story of Al Hafed, an otherwise contented and wealthy farmer in ancient Persia, who searched high and low to find a diamond mine, only to discover at the end of his lengthy search that it was in his backyard all along.

The morale of this story is that good things are often close at hand. This fable is a good metaphor to keep in mind if you are a gang cop, educator, corrections official or other professional committed to prevention. Yes, spend time inside and outside of your community in an attempt to influence boys and young men away from gangs. But don't do so at the expense of protecting and cultivating the diamonds in your backyard – girls and young women. Rest assured that gang members know where the diamonds are, so you'd just better get there first.

As a father of two beautiful girls, I have always protected my gifts. I remember always that the real issue regarding gangs and girls is what gang members do to the lives of young girls. I have never believed that my family was immune just because I was a gang cop. I always took the time to prepare my daughters for what was ahead and made them realize that even at a very young age, the decisions they made were meaningful and could have

150

lifelong consequences. I didn't salt them away and watch over their every move 24-hours a day, I just taught my girls how to think so that they could protect themselves.

If you are a father, spend time with your daughter. If you are a mother, be a positive role model and a shining example to your daughter. If you are a woman without a daughter, invest time in being a good example to a young girl who is close to you. In short, do whatever you can to protect and cultivate the acres of diamonds in *your* backyard.

22

Dealing With The "We Have No Gangs" Syndrome

If I had eight hours to chop down a tree, I'd spend six sharpening my axe.

ABRAHAM LINCOLN

Gangs are a bad thing. They are bad for business, bad for the real estate market, bad for tourism, bad for a school district, bad for politicians, and bad for the community. No one wants them. Many don't even want to admit they have them in their jurisdiction, despite clear evidence to the contrary.

One of the greatest pressures facing professionals who work gangs can be the lack of acknowledgment of the problem. The denial of gang activity often comes from one of several sources, such as your Police Chief, Police Commission, Mayor's office, school administration or local politicians. After all, few community leaders want to admit to the onset or growth of a problem as cancerous as street gangs on their "watch". Their failure to acknowledge the gang issue can create great frustration for you, and may even discourage you from trying to do something about it.

Officers based in Los Angeles, Chicago and New York likely have never experienced this form of denial because of the long and fabled history of gangs in these cities. But in my travels across North America, I have spoken with countless officers and professionals who are forced to deal with the "we have no gangs" syndrome. For some, the lack of sensitivity on the part of the powers-that-be is so disturbing that they have even considered other careers; yet for others, it is precisely the fuel that helps take their "game" to the next level.

One thing is for certain: if there is a potential or emerging gang problem in your jurisdiction, no amount of wishful thinking, denial or creative branding will make it go away. Compared to 20 or 25 years ago, there are gangs in places in which most would never have dreamed. To the traditional well-known North American gang city "membership list" of Los Angeles, Chicago and New York, you must now add unfamiliar cities like Peoria, Arizona; Pine Bluff, Arkansas; Smyrna, Georgia; Goshen, Indiana; Petrolia, Ontario, Canada; Council Bluffs, Iowa; Plum Borough, Pennsylvania and 4,516 other North American towns and cities[1]. Just as gangs are not just a law enforcement problem but a people problem, gangs are not just a big city problem but an every-community problem. Wherever people gather and go about their everyday lives, you are likely to have gangs today, or gangs tomorrow. So we all ought to prepare and sharpen our axes, right?

If you are a front-line officer working in a jurisdiction where your superiors and/or community leaders choose not to acknowledge a gang problem which you know exists, don't despair. There is much you can do, but it demands a patient and committed approach.

If you assume that the gang problem will not go away and will only get worse (a safe assumption in most cities), and if no one is listening or heeding your advice, then prepare for a worst case scenario. Much like what we Californians do, prepare yourself as if you are doing so for an inevitable earthquake. Gather and stockpile supplies, develop response procedures, and make contingency plans. If and when the earthquake hits, your preparations will ensure that you aren't running around like a chicken with its head chopped off. You will be the one who knows how

---

[1] According to the 1998 National Youth Gang Survey, Office of Juvenile Justice and Delinquency Prevention, and the 2002 Canadian Police Survey on Youth Gangs, Solicitor General of Canada.

to react to the situation in a sound and effective manner. You have prepared and thought it through.

Before discussing specific preparations you can make, it is essential to understand that you need not be assigned to a dedicated gang unit to take action. One of the reasons why many police departments don't want to acknowledge a gang presence is because they don't want, or have the ability, to allocate the resources necessary to deal with the problem. If you think that you have to be working a gang unit to be effective in dealing with gangs, you're wrong. Many of the best gang cops I meet are not assigned to a gang or other specialized investigative unit. Being assigned to some type of gang unit doesn't make you a gang cop. Being knowledgeable and effective, do.

The first thing you can do to take action is to establish and document a gang presence. Take photographs of graffiti, noting the date, time and location. Graffiti is one of the first pieces of evidence that makes us aware of a gang presence, so keep a book or log of the graffiti and track its frequency, pattern and monikers of key gang members. If you can read and decipher gang graffiti, you will also know gang tattoos when you see them.

You'll also want to locate and document gang members. This can be done in the normal course of your patrol duties as you stop and interview persons who are possibly involved in criminal or suspicious activity. Gang members, of course, involve themselves in criminal activity, so chances are that you will eventually have occasion to conduct interviews of possible members.

If you encounter a gang member who admits gang membership, take the time to ask additional questions. Pay special attention to your demeanor, as it can greatly influence the information flow during a field interview. A down-to-earth, non-authoritative approach generally works best, rather than an arrogant, authoritative attitude, which does not promote co-operation. Just as important with gang members, the more they think you know, the more willing they are to share information Generally, this is either because they don't want to irritate the situation, or they want to feel they aren't really sharing any big secrets because you're already "in the know" and are probably just testing their honesty towards you anyway.

When a gang member admits to belonging to a specific gang, find out how long he's been involved and what his nickname is. Also probe how long that gang has been in existence, along with its history and origin, enemies, allies, geographical boundaries, hangouts, estimated size and ethnic background, among other things. If you don't ask about specific crimes or members, they won't feel as if they are snitching, and they will discuss many of these topics. Even if you don't get it all at once, the more you get, the more you add to your bank of knowledge. The old adage, "The most you get is the most you ask for" reinforces the above point well.

Even when someone admits to gang membership, try to corroborate their admission with gang tattoos, hand signs, gang paraphernalia or photographs. While I don't wear any tattoos, I find that by acting like I admire them, the gang member is normally co-operative in telling me about the meaning of the tattoo's overall design and its component parts including numbers, abbreviations, symbols and initials. The more you know, the more you can discuss. The more you can discuss, the more you will learn.

When I want to ask something that I feel might shut him down or end the interview, I will normally wait until I'm about to leave or release him from detention. If someone is being released in the field, they will normally give you the answer you want just to get rid of you.

When you find one gang member, you'll likely find more. In public, gang members normally hang out with other gang members. It's part of the way they live, trusting only others in their inner circle. After you've made the contact with the first gang member, the others will realize that you are aware of them and often are more open towards you. Generally, they just don't want to be hassled, so they will co-operate to some extent.

At this point, all you've established is the existence of a gang and that is consists of several members, with whom you've made contact. Now, however, you need to establish the fact that they are involved in criminal activity. If they are not involved in criminal activity, then you don't have a problem. If there's no crime, there's no need for law enforcement to get involved with them. When you do have documentation of criminal activity, however, you are in a better position to validate your contention of gang activity in your jurisdiction and therefore justify a focused police response. Try to document the gang-related crime that occurs in your jurisdiction, keep track of crimes committed by gang members, as well as arrests of gang members. Other documentation that helps is field interview cards or their equivalent. For example, officers responding to a fight at a nightclub may interview four gang members who were involved in a dispute with an employee. While no crime was necessarily committed, the gang members were still the source of the law enforcement response, and that should be documented accordingly.

Now you have the evidence that the gang exists. You have photos of graffiti. You know the background of the gang. You have documented actual gang members and corroborated all of this with tattoos, admissions and photos. You have documentation of their criminal activity with crime reports, arrest reports, and field interviews. You probably also have one more thing in your back pocket - the support of the people in the community who are the victims, witnesses and oftentimes the target of gang activity. They can tell your boss that you are right and that gangs are amongst them.

You can have all of this and more, and it still may not be enough for the gang problem to be addressed. At that point, when your superiors, politicians and bosses don't acknowledge the gangs, you must remain steadfast and continue to do what you've been doing. Continue to document, interview, learn more about the gang, discover more gang members and what they are doing. As time passes, be even more knowledgeable and up-to-date on the gang. Gangs don't go away by themselves. They never do. If the problem is left unchecked, it will worsen, therefore providing you with even more proof.

Rest assured though, that sooner or later, the gang or one of its members will do something that centers them on the radar screen. Perhaps the gang commits a crime so heinous that community leaders won't or can't turn the other cheek (such as the killing of a young child by a stray bullet), or they will make the mistake of committing a crime against a notable person, like raping the mayor's daughter, beating up the Chief of Police's son, or carjacking a professional athlete. When one of these things occurs, the press will get involved and the pressure will be on every one who is accountable to the people. When they get pressured, they will look for a remedy because the call from the community will be, "What are you doing about this gang problem?"

It's during the response to a noteworthy crime or incident such as this that you can step forward and offer your expertise, because you've been aware of the problem, have been studying it, and have invested considerable energy documenting it. While everyone else is under the gun, you will step up, solve the crime and locate the perpetrators. You have been saving up and adding to your knowledge for this moment. You were smart enough to plan ahead and anticipate what would eventually occur. To me, its like being the minor league prospect who, due to player injury, is called up to play in the seventh game of the World Series and performs beyond expectation, because he took the time to prepare, practice and believe.

Just because the leaders around you don't admit to a gang problem, this should not prevent you from learning a gang and readying yourself for the big one, because something of significance will eventually happen. This forward-thinking approach is not just about research and preparation, though. It's about leadership and being passionate about the real work of policing in the face of adversity; it's about being patient and seeing the big picture before it unfolds.

While the real victims of the "We Don't Have No Gangs Syndrome" are the people of the community, take great comfort in knowing that one day, you can give them a sense of hope that someone knowledgeable is on the case. After all, that is what being a great gang cop is really all about.

23

Worry Little About Lack of Community Support

There are two kinds of worries: those you can do something about and those you can't. Don't spend any time on the latter.

DUKE ELLINGTON

Police work is stressful enough without having to worry about the things that you have little or no control over, like the lack of community support we sometimes face.

It's natural to concern yourself with things going on around you, but there are only so many hours in the day. More importantly, you only have so much energy, emotion and ability to focus on all the things around you, so it makes sense to think mostly about the issues that directly affect you, or those that you can influence.

Think of it as if you are going through life with a supermarket cart into which you can place all the issues and concerns that impact you. Since the carrying capacity of a shopping cart is finite, you must be selective with respect to what you put into it. Some items will be desirable, but the price will be too high or the packaging too bulky, so you'll choose to leave them on the store shelf. Other items will be just right, so they'll be placed in your cart alongside others that matter to you.

I try to deal with my police life and work with gangs in very much the same manner. New items to concern myself with appear almost every day, but I choose selectively those with which I will deal or put in my cart, to borrow my analogy. Many circumstances and experiences that pass my way don't elicit my passion and simply are not that important to me. One of them is the relative lack of support we receive from the people we are paid to serve.

For instance, I recall the time around the release of rapper Ice-T's 1992 song, "Cop Killer". The song starts off like this:

I got my black shirt on.
I got my black gloves on.
I got my ski mask on.
This shit's been too long.

I got my twelve gauge sawed off.
I got my headlights turned off.
I'm 'bout to bust some shots off.
I'm 'bout to dust some cops off.

Cop killer, better you than me.
Cop killer, fuck police brutality!
Cop killer, I know your family's grievin' (fuck 'em)
Cop killer, but tonight we get even.

Now, being a member of the LAPD, to whom parts of the song indirectly referenced, the song created a storm of controversy amongst my peers. Even a Dallas police group called for a boycott of the Ice-T record, *Body Count*, as well as the album's label, Warner Brothers. Although I realized that the song drew broad outrage across the law enforcement community and was morally wrong, I knew that if anyone was going to put a bullet in me, it probably wasn't going to be Ice-T. I acknowledged the music and was aware of it. But I focused on more important things than organizing a boycott of a song or worrying about how other people felt about my profession.

In police work, there are many negative issues to deal with. Dangerous work conditions and lukewarm support for what we do are inherent in the job. While we likely knew about these things before we got into police work, it doesn't soften the impact

159

any. We know it's a dangerous job because we are called upon to do things that most of the general public doesn't have the nerve to do. We are paid to stick our noses where no one else dares. For the most part, this is one of the main reasons that many of us seek out this job.

Maybe we want to know how we will react while staring death in the face. Maybe we have things to prove to ourselves. Maybe it's the feeling of walking proud when someone identifies you as a cop. They may not like you, but deep down they respect you because they know that you don't run away from anything.

The public expects us to take care of the dangerous stuff and not let their clean hands get dirty in the process. That's why they pay us so well, as compared to other segments of the working world. Our pay and benefits are all that society is required to provide us. Don't let public support, or the lack of it disturb you. It has always been that way for the cop. That's why this career is so much of a challenge. The odds are against us. Don't dwell on the negative issues and take things personally. You are still important, and you know it.

This is an important lesson to take to heart. Despite the real danger that is inherent in law enforcement, in most cases it is not the major difficulties or disasters that undermine our initiative and passion for the job. It's all the little things that people do – "death by a thousand cuts" – that over time brings out the worst in us and make us question our career choice. It's the citizen who bitches and moans when they get a ticket they know they deserve, the crime victim you saved from serious harm who says you should have gotten there sooner, the politician who says that police are overpaid and ought to do more with less, and the group of youths who say "oink" when you're barely out of earshot. These and other little things often can, over time, generate overwhelming resentment and poison your attitude.

I have found that one of the most effective things I can do to short-circuit these feelings is to identify, by way of simple checklists, the things that I care about, really care about, versus the things that I do not. Consider these two lists:

Things I am concerned about:

- The drunk driver in the next lane
- The guy in the ski mask walking up behind me at the ATM
- The police garage not servicing my vehicle properly
- My immediate supervisor
- The thing crawling in my plate of pork fried rice
- The dog who is foaming at the mouth and growling at my leg
- My child's science project which is due tomorrow morning
- Whether the guy in the black Chevy matching the description of a violent murderer is actually the guy we are after
- Gaining the respect of my police peers and even gang members

Things I don't worry about:

- Whether the academy is as tough as it was when I was there
- Why kids listen to gangster rap stuff
- Why the Rams went to St. Louis
- Who'll be the next president
- Who will win the best actor award this year
- Why my boy won't put down the toilet seat
- Why the lady in front of me has 13 items in the 10-item line at the market
- Airplane turbulence
- Citizens who don't appreciate what I do or what it takes to be a good cop

As you can see, there is quite a difference between the two lists. The problem that we often encounter, however, is that we tend to mix items from both lists together, which increases our emotional burden. But cops are tough, and we can take on the world, right? Wrong! Be smart, and selective with what you place in your cart.

This reminds me of the time I was a young puppy working with a wise and battle-scarred veteran street cop. We were driving down the street at about 4 a.m. and although this was a tough and gang infested neighborhood, it was totally quiet and peaceful on this early morning weekday.

As the veteran was driving he looked at the modest homes lining the dark street. He suddenly pulled over the police car and said to me, "Remember them. Remember the people who are sleeping safely in their homes that you'll never get to meet. You are here risking your butt for them but you'll never see them. They need and want you to be here. They may not be in a position or too afraid to show you. Some cops tend to forget that they are here."

For your own well-being, your focus and concern must be on the things that personally affect or impact you. It's easy to adopt a perception that the community or public doesn't support you in your mission. If you ever feel that way, I suggest a simple trip to your communications division to witness the calls for police service which prove otherwise.

If they didn't want us, they wouldn't call us.

24

It Takes a Community

For a community to be whole and healthy, it must be based on people's love and concern for each other.

MILLARD FULLER

I was born and raised in Los Angeles and have either worked or lived in the city my entire life. I don't have a Master's degree in sociology, nor have I conducted extensive research on the relationship between police and the community. However, I have seen enough pain, human suffering and unhappiness in 51 years to have a good grasp of the police/community relations problem and its primary issues.

Police/community relations is a complex matter. In my front row seat I've seen glimpses of what works, and ample evidence of what does not. I will soon leave the front lines of policing and will eventually move on with my life, but the thoughts contained in this chapter, I hope, will be my enduring contribution to improving the manner in which police and the community relate to one another. To some, these ideas may seem radical or impractical, but I ask you to try and keep an open mind. Societal problems like gangs, drugs and poor community/police relations have been around for years and seem to be getting worse (or at least not improving), so perhaps there *is* a better way.

It is a fundamental truism that the police officer and the criminal element exist in an adversarial relationship. When people commit crimes, and at the same time generate community support or at least engender a sense of indifference, the cop becomes the bad guy. There will always be gang members who see themselves as representatives or guardians of the neighborhood, who freely proclaim that they exist to fight the evils of "those dogs that oppress us". Unfortunately, in communities where there is little sense of hope and true leadership, people sometimes buy into this mutated role reversal.

Contrasting this is law enforcement, which society at large entrusts to keep order in the community. We know that in some communities throughout North America, if it weren't for the police, things would be in total chaos. No one would be safe. We know and see ourselves as saviors and protectors.

It's no wonder, therefore, that there are police/community relations problems. We in law enforcement see ourselves as protectors, while some communities see us as the enemy. This creates distrust and misunderstanding.

Management theories abound in policing, and one of the latest catch phrases is "problem solving". Problem solving doesn't mean problem attending, problem acknowledging or problem noticing. Although it may be a well-meaning gesture on the part of a new captain, superintendent or commanding officer, showing up at a community meeting in a crisply pressed uniform to shake hands while promising change and passing out balloons does not solve problems. It may be a start, but many times, that's the extent of actual problem solving in the community as far as the role of the law enforcement is concerned, and it does little to *actually* improve the quality of life in these neighborhoods.

Thankfully, there are officers out there who are busting their asses and doing more than their share of actual problem-solving in the communities they serve to make them better places to live. I believe that we can learn from their vision and passion and all do more to improve communities in general, and the relationship between police and communities specifically.

In the old days, we could get away with saying, "I'm not a social worker" or "that's your parents' problem, not mine." The truth of the matter is that as the family structure continues to break down, law enforcement professionals must do more. The first thing we can do is change the general attitude regarding community relations.

I have been on numerous interview boards for candidates attempting to enter the Los Angeles Police Department. One phase of the selection process is the oral interview where the applicant addresses a panel made up of law enforcement officers and members of the community. The oral interview allows the candidate to showcase him or herself and answer questions regarding his/her background, aspirations and suitability for the job.

On almost all of the boards I sat on, the candidate mentioned that one of the reasons that he or she wants to be a cop is to give back to the community and make society a better place. Somewhere down the line, however, giving back to the community gets lost in the shuffle of radio calls, stressful situations, arrests of dangerous criminals and long challenging work days.

One reason that it loses its importance is that the unrelenting environment of peer pressure and competition amongst police officers requires them to be strong, brave, macho, tough and tactically proficient. You are constantly compared and scrutinized by your peers and superiors. For a young recruit officer just out of the academy, that creates a boatload of pressure. The young recruit officer emulates what he sees in other officers so that he can be accepted and fit in. Notice that I did not mention caring, compassion or sensitivity as essential qualities. Unfortunately, these qualities are often perceived as weakness in a young officer.

The average street cop is not totally responsible for the generally aggressive mentality that is encouraged and expected toward the community. I was walking through a police station the other day and observed some charts on the bulletin board of a hallway in the open for everyone to see. The charts listed the names of the officers who were in the top ten in the division for various categories such as tickets, felony arrests, warrant checks and radio calls handled. Those charts were on display to reward the officers who ranked highest in the various categories.

The interesting thing about the bulletin board display is that this particular police division probably represents one of the lowest income areas of the city. The division has more than its share of drugs, gangs, violence, crime and social ills, and they're encouraging ticket writing. I'm all for writing a ticket to a gangster or criminal type who needs to learn a lesson, but some of those tickets are being written to the poor guy who is working 12 hours a day for meager earnings, trying to feed his family, and it just so happens that his car has a cracked windshield. In his eyes, you are not a problem solver, you are a problem maker. This guy has to worry about feeding his kids, paying the bills, keeping his family safe in a dangerous neighborhood and hoping the damned car will start in the morning. He now has to worry about you seeing the 2-inch crack in his windshield and signing him up because you want your name on the bulletin board in the hallway of the police station. That's the system in which we're trying to encourage police/community relations.

My department does not demand or enforce a quota system regarding traffic tickets. However, supervisors do hold their subordinates accountable for being "productive". The easiest way for a one-dimensional supervisor to assess the value of his subordinates is to count things. You know, count tickets, arrests, sick days, complaints…you get the picture. Counting things doesn't always tell the story.

I once had a new supervisor approach me while I was working patrol in Newton Street Division and counsel me regarding my lack of traffic ticket writing volume. He wanted to know why I didn't write more tickets in this Division, where there was a high crime rate, plenty of gangs, drugs and violence. I told him that I wrote tickets when I felt it was appropriate. He further informed me that there was no reason that I couldn't write at least two tickets per day.

I told him, "Well something is wrong because I'm not going to. Traffic tickets are a tool that we use to educate the public in traffic safety. I'm not writing more tickets or writing fewer tickets. I write tickets when it's appropriate. Besides, you can't hunt lions and tigers with worms" (he's still trying to figure that one out). Luckily for me, he checked with some of the other supervisors who knew me and they convinced him to leave me alone as there was probably bigger fish to fry than my lack of traffic enforcement. My point is that some of the things we do as patrol officers are encouraged and expected within the system we work in.

As members of the law enforcement community, we must all do more to improve our relationship with the community and therefore earn a reputation as problem solvers. The following analogy will help you understand my proposed solution to the police/community relations problem.

In a restaurant, you have the chef who cooks the food, the waiter or waitress who serves the food and of course, the customer. If you are missing any of these integral parts, you can't operate the restaurant successfully. If I were the ruler of my kingdom, I would have my police force act as the waiters and waitresses of the community. The community-based organizations and resources would be the chefs in the kitchen. The customers of the restaurant are the people in the community in need of the resources and support organizations.

In addition to writing tickets for cracked windshields and loud mufflers, I would also have my officers issue citations (referrals) for things such as lack of food in the home or truant children. Every day, patrol officers walk into homes during radio calls and see a variety of problems not relating to the radio call; problems that are not of a criminal nature, but problems that will eventually plant the seeds for criminal behavior.

Traditionally, we handle the call, say goodbye to everyone and leave. We may have done a good job handling the call, but any other problem in that home will continue to exist even after we leave. That seven year old kid is still hungry, that 15 year old girl is still a high school dropout, that single mother is still an alcoholic, and there is still no food in the house. In a problem solving police force, that is four citations or referrals that my officers should have written.

The referral that is written and given to the recipient (citizen) is nothing more than a phone number to a department sanctioned community-based organization or resource agency that can assist the citizen with the particular problem that he or she is facing. My officers would carry a notebook in their police vehicle that contains a list of sanctioned agencies by particular issue or problem. The notebook would contain, for example, four agencies for tattoo removal, seven food banks and eleven battered women's shelters, among other things. The officers would carry blank referral forms that they would fill out when necessary, much like a traffic ticket. When a referral is completed, the citizen gets a copy along with the department and the involved agency. Upon receipt of the completed referral, the agency would contact the citizen who was referred, assuming that they had not already made contact with the agency for assistance. It is crucial that the involved agency conduct a follow-up to the initial referral, even if the citizen appears non-compliant. The idea is to get the problem solved.

A special community relations unit within my police department would be responsible for screening each agency before putting its seal of approval on it. The reward for the agency is the backing and endorsement of a law enforcement agency and more efficient use of what resources the particular agency has to offer. We would bring the agency more customers, making it more successful in accomplishing its mission. When the involved agency comes up for renewal, a successful program involving the police department increases the chance of additional funding.

The obvious benefit to the citizens is true problem solving by having the on-scene police officers direct them to the appropriate and available resources. Most of the problems that plague a community are not criminal in nature, but if allowed to breed and fester, will eventually lead or contribute to criminal activity.

Police officers in this scenario are the waiters and waitresses, and they are the most logical people in society to play these roles. Cops are the ones on the scene, out all hours of the day and night. The police department never closes. We see people in their natural environment. We witness first hand the embryonic causes of crime. We are expert problem sensors. As first responders, we can become the expert problem solvers, or at minimum, the catalysts for problems to be addressed.

What's in it for the individual officer? Many of the rough and tumble cops I know who work crime-ridden and violent areas do so because they know that in those areas, the people really need them. No matter how much crime and violence exists in a community, the majority of people are law abiding and good-hearted. They want a safe and happy life. I know that in many inner city neighborhoods in L.A., it's not unusual to see street cops buying ice cream for little kids or shooting a basketball with the local teenagers. It's just not publicized. My point is that if those officers could do more, they probably would. The system has never consistently encouraged it. As front line officers, we are the ones who are faced with the angry and frustrated citizenry who expect more from us because they have been promised it.

One of the real benefits to the individual officer in my proposed system is the fact that copies of the completed referrals would be tabulated and maintained by the department. Those referrals could be considered when decisions are made regarding promotions, assignments and discipline, much like negative issues are currently compiled. For example, it would be difficult to prove an allegation that you are a discourteous or racist police officer when the records shows that in the past 6 months, you completed 72 referrals to the citizens in the community that you serve. So there is reward beyond the personal satisfaction you will gain by genuinely helping others. If you can imagine that you have actually completed that many referrals, that's 72 positive, problem solving and meaningful referrals. If another officer sees the same problem at the same location that you saw six months earlier, he can refer it again. Obviously, there's still a problem.

This citation-based problem solving approach requires that the police department brass buy into this system and therefore reward the problem solvers. If they were to do so and systematize the process right from the academy level forward, all police officers eventually would buy into the process. For new recruits who are constantly coming on stream, if they want the job, they'll do it the way we want them to do it. That has never changed.

The benefit to the police department is that the cost involved is minimal. The many agencies and resources seeking clients already exist. We are merely being more effective in pointing those in need in the right direction. We are also pointing the concerned agencies in the right direction and making better use of them. There would be the cost of creating and printing the referral forms and a department coordinator would have to be selected, whose duty it would be to select, research and monitor the prospective agencies. He would also ensure the completed forms are distributed properly and that the follow-up contacts are done in a timely manner.

In support of this system, training would also be given department-wide on the root causes of criminal behavior so that the officers would know what to look for. The training would help them in making better decisions regarding referrals. Some may laugh and say that it's ridiculous to try and train officers and make them social workers. I think that it's ridiculous that we allow officers to walk into unstable and volatile situations with little knowledge of basic criminology concepts such as risk and protective factors.

In relation to gangs, this process would put the police department on the point as far as gang prevention and intervention are concerned. As front line officers, we are the point men because we see gang members before they become gang members. We see them before anyone else does. We see them before the first tattoo, before the new moniker, before their first brush with the law.

The overall reward is that we would no longer be seen as marauding invaders in the neighborhood only there to harass and screw with people. We would help people, make meaningful connections and break down some of the unfair stereotypes connected with the police. If we expect community support, we have to support the community.

There will always be crime and violence. There will also always be victims, and sometimes the victims will be us, the law enforcement officer. We can never prevent this entirely but we can certainly slant the odds in our favor. The more support we get from the community, the safer we will be as front line cops.

In my vision, some day soon in the future a gangster will tell an officer, "We don't want or need you down here. All you guys do is mess with people". That officer will then turn to the gang member and say, "Hey, I've completed 72 referrals in the last six months down here in your neighborhood. Two of those got your little brothers and sisters food and clothes, you dumb ass."

25

I Guess I Didn't Need It

Press on: nothing in the world can take the place of persever-
ance. Talent will not; nothing is more common than unsuccess-
ful men with talent. Genius will not; unrewarded genius is almost
a proverb. Education will not; the world is full of educated dere-
licts. Persistence and determination alone are omnipotent.

CALVIN COOLIDGE

By the latter part of 1985, I had completed almost five years of service in the Los Angeles Police Department's Gang Detail. Driving my bright yellow Plymouth Fury police car, affectionately known as the Pacman car, my job was to develop information on gangs in order to help various divisional detectives solve crimes and track down and arrest the suspects, mostly violent gang members.

At that time, my partner and I had been looking for several months for a gang member wanted on at least two murders, probably more. Our intelligence suggested that he was using co-caine very heavily and was extremely violent and aggressive. He had become so dangerous and unpredictable that he was not even trusted by his fellow gang members.

Fortunately, I had an informant in that particular gang who was feeding me information on our suspect. The suspect had threatened the informant with death and was acting in an impul-sive and violent manner. The informant knew that our suspect was wanted for murder, so he figured that the best way to rid himself of the violent threat to his life was to lead us to him so that we could put him in prison.

One day, my informant contacted me and told me that the suspect was hiding in an apartment building in South-Central Los Angeles on Colden Avenue. I was warned that the suspect had just picked up an Uzi and was looking to kill my partner and I, as he knew we were looking for him in that "stupid yellow car".

The informant also told me that our suspect had stolen a car and had parked it on 95th Street, one block north of Colden Avenue. According to our informant, when leaving the apartment the suspect would exit the rear of the apartment, climb the fence and then head north which would then give him access to 95th Street and the parked stolen car. He would then repeat the process in the reverse when returning home. The informant's insight was valuable, as was his last warning: "Bring all of your guys... he's gonna go out the hard way and try to take you with him".

Armed with this time-sensitive information, we gathered our men together and supplemented it with some extra officers, so that our take-down squad totalled fourteen. We had a very long briefing at Southeast Station to discuss the suspect, the updated information we had on him and our strategy to apprehend him. Our briefing was particularly lengthy because the suspect was extremely dangerous and the officers had a lot of good ideas as to how to apprehend him. Overall, the briefing was very insightful and constructive and we developed a strategy with which we were all comfortable.

The plan was for a small contingent of officers, "pointmen", to secretly watch the front of the apartment to let everyone know when the possible suspect exited the apartment and proceeded to the rear of the building. At that point, anticipating that he was headed for the next street north, we'd move undercover officers in unmarked police vehicles to 95th Street where the stolen car was parked. When he went to his car, we'd converge on him with our cars, trapping him like a fish in a fish bowl and preventing the car from leaving. We knew that as it got darker through the day, we'd be able to get up on him quickly.

We had been on the surveillance for a few hours and it was dark. There had been little activity except for a guy sticking his head out of one of the apartments and quickly sticking it back in. Hours passed and not much had happened, but that one guy did give us some encouragement.

All of a sudden, one of our pointmen stated, "I have a male coming out of one of the apartments. He looks good as a possible for our suspect. He just walked to the rear of the apartment building."

As I was going to be a driver of one of the cars blocking in the suspect in the stolen car, I moved north up Hoover Avenue (which ran perpendicular to the west of 95th and Colden) to 95th Street. My lights were out and I was waiting for any vehicle lights to turn on. We had other officers parked on the darkened street so we were also waiting for their direction.

One of the pointmen blurted out, "We have a small yellow vehicle coming out from the front of the apartment building and exiting onto Colden." My yellow car was facing northbound on Hoover Avenue at 95th Street ready to make a right turn east onto 95th. This change in plans would now put the suspect behind us on Colden so I quickly made a U-turn and creeped southbound along Hoover Avenue towards Colden Avenue. The pointman then stated, "The vehicle is coming westbound along Colden towards Hoover. It's him! It's him!"

Since I knew I would soon cross paths with the suspect, I waited to see what he was going to do in his car. My adrenaline was rising as I sat somewhat exposed on the well-lit Hoover Avenue in the yellow Plymouth Fury with my temporary partner for the evening (a supervisor no less - my regular partner was one of the pointmen secreted in front of the apartment building).

The yellow Datsun B-210 with the suspect driving got to Hoover and began to make a right turn north turn towards us. In the middle of his turn, his vehicle stopped abruptly and the turn signal that had been activated was turned off. His headlights were on and their beams were directed right at us, lighting us up. He had to have seen us in the Pacman car.

Feeling like sitting ducks with his headlights blinding us, I needed to make a decision. My only option, I believed, was to ram him head on with the Pacman car, otherwise be riddled with

Uzi rounds through our windshield. I thought that since my Plymouth Fury was bigger and heavier than his Datsun B-210, that turning Pacman into a ramrod would be an effective offensive decision.

I yelled "hang on …!" to my partner and floored the Plymouth toward the suspect. The move caught our suspect by surprise because his car lunged forward westbound in the middle of the intersection in order to avoid us. Our car nailed the right rear quarter panel of his car with our right front bumper. As he was trying to escape by racing westbound on Colden Avenue, I could see him holding the Uzi in his right hand with the barrel facing up while he steered with his left hand. I didn't hit the suspect's car the way I wanted to, but the impact made him lose control of his car and it came to a rest in the middle of the intersection diagonally, facing in a southwest direction.

After I hit him, I turned my car sharply to the right so we were facing westbound in the middle of the intersection, about 50 feet directly in front of the driver's door of the suspect's Datsun. Suddenly, the suspect exited his vehicle, holding the Uzi with both hands. It was the same face I had been staring at in pictures for the past few months. He raised the Uzi as if to begin to fire his weapon, and once again I stomped on the gas pedal of the Pacman car, forcefully slamming him back into the little yellow car. I then jumped out of my car and heard numerous gunshots as I scrambled to the rear of my police car.

As I crouched behind my Fury, I recalled from my training the story of a California Highway Patrol officer who was shot and killed during a gunfight while he was at the rear of his vehicle reloading. I decided that I wasn't going out that way without a fight. I pulled my gun out and moved forward along the driver's side of my vehicle. I could see the suspect seated facing away from me in his vehicle. Shots were going off and it appeared that he was exchanging shots with someone outside the passenger door of his vehicle. He couldn't see me. He was looking at them, whoever it was.

The shots continued and the suspect was moving. I took steady aim and squeezed the trigger of my Smith & Wesson .38

caliber revolver, putting one shot perfectly in the back of the suspect's head. I knew it was a perfect shot because as it entered the suspect, I could see his head move in a synchronized reaction to my shot. The shots ceased. The suspect stopped moving. One of our guys jumped into the vehicle and handcuffed the bullet-riddled suspect.

As we later learned, the suspect had been shot over 20 times and had gotten off only one shot, probably at us when the Pacman car raced towards him the second time. I was amazed at the swiftness and bravery displayed by the other members of the squad who approached the armed suspect immediately after my car hit him the second time. Those outgunned officers ran up to the suspect's vehicle and engaged the armed suspect. Their actions prevented the suspect from exiting his vehicle and doing damage to all of us.

In the aftermath, we determined that the suspect was en route to Inglewood to kill a witness. The perfect shot I thought I took from the side of my vehicle was actually taken through the inside of the front windshield of our yellow police car. I was so focused on the back of the suspect's head that I didn't realize that I was trying to shoot through the windshield. And my perfect shot that I thought entered the back of the suspect's head actually ricocheted off the windshield and nestled itself safely into the engine block of the Pacman car. So much for my perfect shot.

As a result of the ensuing crime scene investigation, interviews and medical treatment at the local emergency hospital for the numerous bruises I received during the two collisions, I did not get back to Parker Center (my station) until 8 a.m., some eleven hours after the shooting the night before. Needless to say, it was one long night, but everything worked out well for us as we got our guy.

I was at my desk readying myself to go home when I was approached by a seasoned and well-respected detective I had known for years. He said to me, "I heard about your caper last night. Everyone says you did a hell of a job."

The comment meant a lot to me because I respected the detective, and knew he had been involved in several shootings as well. While I wasn't pleased about the resting place of my "perfect shot", he assured me that what I had done was courageous and probably saved the lives of some of our officers. The missed shot was not that big a deal to him. Rather, my actions with the police car under duress were.

Then he said to me, "You'll get the medal for this!" He was referring to the Los Angeles Police Department's Medal of Valor, the highest award the department can bestow on an officer. The Medal of Valor is very prestigious and you simply cannot plan your career around winning it. To win it, an officer has to find themselves in a real life and death situation and respond appropriately. While I've always felt that most officers on our department would rise to the occasion if presented with such a situation, few ever get the opportunity. I have complete respect for all Medal of Valor recipients, many of whom were wounded in the line of duty or won the award posthumously.

As the months rolled by, from time to time I would hear others mention the Medal of Valor award in connection with my actions and those of others during the shooting at the intersection of Hoover and Colden. Sometimes, I would catch myself thinking about how nice it would be to receive the award, especially in front of my parents and family. I never set out to win the award, but I was now thinking what an honor it would be to be a recipient.

Almost a year after the incident, my captain called me into his office and informed me that he had bad news. I was not going to receive the Medal of Valor. He went on to say that although my actions were worthy of the award and prevented myself and other officers from being hurt or killed, the department didn't want to encourage other officers to use their police vehicles as weapons. I felt it was an unfair decision and that each incident should be judged on its own merit. I was disappointed, but indeed, I had set myself up for that disappointment by thinking about how I would feel if I won it.

Disappointed as I was, I didn't go on a hunger strike, work stoppage or develop an unhealthy attitude. I didn't let that "perceived injustice" affect the person or cop I wanted to be. I continued to be productive and happy as a Los Angeles Police officer. I rationalized that for me, the Medal of Valor wasn't meant to be. In my mind, I concluded simply that "I guess I didn't need it."

Fast forward 15 years. In 2001, I was deployed as supervisor of the same squad I worked within for five years while driving the yellow Pacman police car. In those intervening fifteen years, I worked at Narcotics Division, Organized Crime and Intelligence Division, Northeast Division Detectives and a brief stint at West L.A. Division right after the O.J. Simpson murder investigation. I had also spent a year back on loan to the Gang Detail in 1989. Those fifteen years were marked with good times and bad, ups and downs, and the typical emotional and spiritual roller coaster ride that is commonplace in law enforcement. But at the end of the fifteen years I made it back to the squad I once loved working. I was now supervising that squad. I had my dream job.

During my time in that Gang Detail as a police officer, I had a lieutenant who was now, fifteen years later, the captain of the division overseeing the same gang unit. When I was selected for the supervisory position, he told me in private that he wanted me to run the unit in the same manner we worked in the 1980s. He wanted a specialized, proactive squad that went out and hunted down violent gang members and career criminals, the worst of the worst. When I got to the squad, it was basically an administrative unit that worked on providing the department statistics on gang related crime and providing some gang training. With the addition of several key detectives and officers, we developed into an extremely efficient group of cops who could go into any gang area or neighborhood in Los Angeles and surgically remove the violent threat from the community. A divisional detective would investigate a case like a murder or robbery and when the case was solved, the detective would contact us to go out and apprehend the identified suspect.

Through the years, we consistently did high quality and dangerous work. The suspects were always the most dangerous and violent. Over and over again, we'd hunt them down and successfully bring them in with a minimum amount of trouble. We weren't bringing in a high number of arrests, but we were bringing in significant ones. It was quality, not quantity. With the type of criminals we were dealing with, you weren't going to apprehend them in high numbers. They were the most seasoned, wily and experienced criminals who were experts at eluding arrest. These were big fish and it took awhile to get them into the boat. My guiding philosophy was part and parcel of our work - it's not how *much* you do, it's *what* you do.

By 1999, we had firmly established ourselves as one of the most productive and skilled squads in the LAPD. We had also been called upon to conduct surveillance and field operations on sensitive, confidential and high profile cases not involving gangs. We were proficient as a unit, but we were low key, maybe too low key, a situation which was not helped by the fact that our unit's name was changed twice.

During this time, I had been approached a couple of times by my superiors regarding the idea of our squad being showcased on reality TV shows like *Cops* and *LAPD ... Life on the Street*. I had seen numerous squads like ours on cop shows, documentaries and news features highlighting their exploits. Many times, certain tactics and methods were exposed for their entertainment value for all to see, including criminals. In all my years of police work, I had yet to see a street gang produce a training video that detailed their tactics, methods and mentality and then broadcast it to law enforcement professionals. I was hesitant about sharing our unit's specialized tactics with the criminal element. While I thought that highlighting patrol officers doing their job was entertaining and demonstrative of how difficult their job is, showing the unique methods of specialized units was different. So, I turned down these offers because I thought it would divulge too much information about our unit, making a difficult job even more so. I thought that it would work against us, and the price we paid was lack of notoriety.

As a squad, we had been told on a few occasions by our superiors that we were going to be submitted for the Los Angeles Police Department Unit Citation for the collective work we had done. We waited and waited, but no commendation was forthcoming. I had my dream job and didn't want to be promoted or work elsewhere. While I didn't need the "spiritual income" that was part of a unit commendation, my squad deserved it. I also felt that for some of them, the commendation would be welcomed because the fine job they were doing was becoming somewhat thankless. The commendation was offered up to us as a carrot and we felt we deserved it. This feeling was particularly acute, since other officers and squads around us were getting accolades for doing things that were not as difficult or significant as our work. Our squad deserved the recognition from its peers.

We waited longer and still no commendation. When none of our superiors would write it for us, I decided to write and submit the commendation myself. I highlighted our many accomplishments in 1999, including significant incidents and arrests and included the amount of time we took to develop and administer gang training to our fellow department employees. The commendation looked real good and got submitted up the line to the commendation board.

Several months passed and we received no word about the unit citation. Still more months passed and we finally learned that the commendation board never received the commendation that was written. It had been lost ... gone ... disappeared. We were instructed to submit it again.

Now that almost another year had passed, I added our 2000 accomplishments to our 1999 ones to even better justify the unit citation. In the commendation I had written, there were 35 separate examples of outstanding judgment, tactics and teamwork while capturing extremely dangerous criminals. Our administrative unit was also included in the commendation, as they had trained over 1,000 department employees in the use of CAL-GANG, the newly adopted state-wide gang database.

We also reflected in the commendation that, collectively, our squad had designed and delivered a series of one-day

CRASH school sessions because our 300+ gang officers were receiving no additional training as gang officers. This training was something we developed for their good and was not even mandated. If we hadn't done it, no one would have cared enough to do it for the officers. When the Chief of Police later abolished the CRASH units because of the Rampart Division scandal, we came to the rescue and provided gang training to over 400 officers now assigned to the newly formed "Special Enforcement Units" that replaced the CRASH units. If these accomplishments were not enough, I also highlighted the fact that our squad put in many long hours in the hot sun working a special assignment during the 2000 Democratic National Convention that was held in Los Angeles. It was one of many special missions that our squad was tasked with, performing in an outstanding manner during all of them.

I submitted the commendation and a few months later, we were informed that we would not receive a unit citation. Our accomplishments were not worthy of the award. On the inside, I was angered by the commendation board's decision. They either didn't read or understand the amount of exceptional work we had accomplished. To show the degree of the injustice involved in the commendation board's decision, one of the members of our unit showed me a commendation his unit received a few years back, which centered on a single outstanding arrest. It was indeed an outstanding arrest by his old unit, but it would have amounted to only one of the 35 incidents I had detailed in our commendation. They had no other activities involved with their award. We had hours and hours of training development and administration to hundreds of officers. We were also called upon to complete specialized and sensitive assignments that we did in an exemplary manner.

I gathered my emotions and shared the bad news with the squad. I let them know how I felt because I wasn't going to give them a company line about "it just wasn't good enough". We all knew that we deserved it. Despite how I felt about that board, I gave each of our squad members a copy of the commendation I had written. I wanted them to share it with their families, friends and loved ones. I wanted them to feel appreciated by the people who were important to them.

Although we considered the lack of recognition a setback, we weren't going to let our disappointment detract from what we had accomplished through the years as a team. We were not going to let it take away from the accomplishments yet to be made. I wasn't going to allow it as a supervisor. The people in our squad weren't going to allow it, as members of a team composed of high moral character. The commendation board's blindness wasn't going to break my spirit or the collective spirit of the squad. We had worked too long and too hard, and we were too committed to our work and to each other.

To this day as a squad we have continued on in our quiet and effective way, removing the most violent criminals and gang members from the community. We are larger and more effective than we have ever been. If you were to look us up, as of the writing of this book, we are the "Gang Field Unit" of the "Gang Support Section" of the "Special Operation Support Division" of the Los Angeles Police Department. We are still in business.

I made a decision many years ago to take personal disappointment and turn it into fuel that would drive an even higher level of achievement. Faced with the same disappointment as a supervisor of a high impact squad that I experienced years earlier as a Pacman driving front line cop, I attempted to deal with the situation the same way, by not letting it consume me or my people and our passion for the job. I am proud to say that collectively, we took that snub as a challenge and did not allow it to detract from the enjoyment we derive from our job and the time we spend together as a team. We know that true satisfaction comes from good quality and consistent work, and the respect and goodwill that come from *within* our unit.

One last thing; if you happen to be one of the members of that commendations board that refused to acknowledge our accomplishments, don't worry about your error in judgment. I guess we just didn't need it.

26
The Most Important Lesson

This is the true joy in life, being used for a purpose recognized by yourself as a mighty one. Being a force of nature instead of a feverish, selfish little clod of ailments and grievances complaining that the world will not devote itself to making you happy. I am of the opinion that my life belongs to the whole community and as I live it is my privilege - my **privilege** *to do for it whatever I can. I want to be thoroughly used up when I die, for the harder I work the more I love. I rejoice in life for its own sake. Life is no brief candle to me; it is a sort of splendid torch which I've got a hold of for the moment and I want to make it burn as brightly as possible before handing it on to future generations."*

GEORGE BERNARD SHAW

There are a number of reasons why I wrote this book. My motivation was not monetary. If it were, I would not have geared this book to such a specific audience. Rather, I would have structured my writing towards the general public, since many of the lessons presented in this book can be applied outside the world of law enforcement and gangs.

I wrote this book because after 28 years of working in a high stress, competitive and dangerous world, I am able to laugh, smile and have a good time while continuing to be productive and content. I look around and see friends, colleagues and fellow law enforcement professionals who have fallen by the wayside because of misfortune, stress, bitterness and self-destruction. I have also seen those who have maintained a healthy attitude but are stricken with medical and physical setbacks.

While I have experienced my fair share of adversity, which is part and parcel of the world of policing, I know I am fortunate to be in my leadership situation, still with a positive frame of mind.

Indeed, there are many things I feel fortunate about. We in law enforcement have a tendency to be negative, cynical and callous. We've been duped into believing that that's how to survive the pressures of law enforcement, as if a tough external shell is all that is required to stay safe. That may be one way, but it's certainly not my way. When I start to fall into a funk or a negative mindset, I count my blessings. Here's what I mean.

I'm fortunate that I remain passionate about my work after 28 years of hard service. I'm fortunate that I have the ability to go to work and laugh in the face of evil. I don't do that as a cocky super hero, but because I am confident in my abilities and those of my dedicated team members, and our expertise to meet the challenges thrust our way.

I also laugh because I'm amused at the criminal or gang member's perception of a "warrior". A bully is not a warrior. A person who cowardly fires a gun and runs away and hides is not a warrior. A warrior puts food on the table for his family and hides his fear for the sake of his loved ones. A warrior never runs away because it's not in his composition. Tattoos, muscles and guns don't make a warrior. Spirit, loyalty and responsibility do. I know that as my adversary pretends to be a warrior, that I *am* a warrior, and that makes me smile.

I'm fortunate for having the confidence and wisdom to make a decision and learn from it, right or wrong. My confidence comes from being well trained, cared for and encouraged. My confidence comes from those I have confidence in as they have confidence in me. My decisiveness comes from experience, focus and stability. I have also learned that making no decision is sometimes worse than making the wrong one. It also comes from knowing that an honest effort produces success most of the time. Those are the best odds you can get.

I'm fortunate for having my moments alone in the dark without fear because of my strength and the strength of those around me. I can be weak and discourage myself or I can be strong and encourage myself. Most of the time I'm strong and that's good. Life continues on in stages and even the bad days eventually go away. I may not always be able to defeat those bad days, but I can certainly endure them long enough for another day.

I am fortunate because I have the sense not to beat myself up over work, relationships or failures. As long as I'm busy taking action, I recognize that failures will surface. But, as long as I'm sincere in my effort, I know I can deal with the failure. Even if I fail, I know I will remain loyal to myself, and I feel fortunate for that. I maintain my dignity, self-respect and character because those qualities supersede any rank, class or organizational structure. I once had a captain chew me out for some irrelevant reason – maybe he had seen too many cop shows on TV where the superior officers treated their subordinates like crap. I told him, "Don't talk to me that way. Only one person can talk to me like that and that's my father. You're not my father." I understand and respect the rank structure in law enforcement, but relinquishing my dignity will never be part of the equation.

I am fortunate because I have maintained my compassion for kids, the elderly and the weak. I know that they are principally the reason we risk our lives on a daily basis. I know that without law enforcement and its heroes, youth, the elderly and the weak would have a more brutal existence. While I can still carry my own groceries, drive my car and find my way home, I don't take these things for granted because one day I will only have the fading memories of my younger days. I remind myself that there are ordinary kids out there living a life that no one deserves; kids who sleep on the floor, go to bed hungry, enjoy no love or support, experience violence daily, and skip school because they have no clean clothes to wear. I feel fortunate because I work for the children who can't stand up to bullies but must, on a day to day basis, face them alone. I feel fortunate because I live and breathe the reality that in this wild and chaotic world, we are leaders in the community and are the strong ones. I know that we cannot cheat the young, the weak or the elderly, as that would be cheating ourselves.

I am fortunate because I have surrounded myself with a supportive network of family, friends, co-workers and loved ones who have come to expect much from me but remain loyal when their expectations aren't met. There's an old saying that goes something like this: "You never want to be in a position where you have to find out who you're real friends are." I have been in that position and know who they are. I hope that I am considered a true friend to them as well.

I'm also comforted in the knowledge that despite whatever may occur at work, my relationship with my kids never changes. I am fortunate that I can have a private, personal conversation with each of them and know that love, trust and respect was instilled in them through the years. I will always have somewhere where I belong.

I am fortunate that I have maintained my sense of humor. My sense of humor has always been my ice-breaker, my shield and my nerve settler. When I'm laughing I am comfortable. When I'm comfortable, I'm at my best. My sense of humor has allowed me to better enjoy the law enforcement adventure and remind me that's all it is - an adventure. My sense of humor cuts through stress, tension and fear. My sense of humor feeds off the humor of others making the job more enjoyable. I don't laugh because I'm goofy, I laugh because I'm happy. I also remember that happy kids don't join gangs.

I am fortunate that I can exist without being at work. I can go to a Kings hockey game, a Barnes and Noble bookstore or get nostalgic and smile while listening to Peter Frampton delivering "Baby I Love Your Way" just one more time. I can sit and watch the UCLA-USC football game and wonder what my dad thinks of the game from heaven. I can be "big and fat" to my eldest grandson because his hugs and kisses are as pure as the sun setting on the Pacific Ocean. I can blush with pride each time my youngest grandson holds his arms out for his big and ugly grandpa to hold him. I can be alone and realize that being alone is not a curse or imperfection, as it can be one of life's most precious rewards.

I am fortunate because as a law enforcement professional, I have had the pleasure of meeting and working alongside some of the best people in the world. It doesn't matter if it's the Los Angeles Police Department, the Los Angeles County Sheriff's Department, the NYPD, the California Department of Corrections, the New Jersey State Police, the Ottawa Police Service, the ATF or any other agency, it is pride, integrity and a sense of duty that abound and sustain me. It doesn't matter if it's a sworn officer or a civilian, a homicide detective or a correctional officer, a probation officer or a prosecutor, educator or community volunteer, there are quality people everywhere who have taken up the law enforcement mission. People are what they are on the inside. Uniforms, titles and rank are just the crust or outer shell. The most admirable part is within, and it is there, plain to see, if you only take the time to look for it.

My purpose in writing this chapter was to demonstrate that I am just like you. I wrote this chapter to remind you that you are also fortunate, sometimes more fortunate than you realize. You are working in a profession that many aspire to, but few achieve. You are fortunate because you have the wherewithal and drive to read books like this one, so as to improve who you are and the service your provide to the community. And you are fortunate because like me, you are alive, and you are making a contribution to your fellow man.

In this way, I am no different than most of you. Any of you can write this chapter by inserting your own personal themes and perspectives. I just happen to be very conscious of the negative threats that exist all around us due to our mission. I have used my own strategy to deal with it. I have learned *how* to be happy.

More than learning how to be happy, I have allowed myself to simply *be* happy. Of everything I have said or will ever say, this is the final and most important *Lesson From A Gang Cop.*

Acknowledgements

Most people live in a very restricted circle of their potential being. We all have reservoirs of energy and genius to draw upon of which we do not dream.

WILLIAM JAMES

The following people have had an impact on me during my life and career in law enforcement.

For each person named, there are many more that go unmentioned, but to have done so would have required a whole other book. A heartfelt thanks to everyone for their support, encouragement and friendship.

Refugio Aguilar
Jessica Almeraz
Nelson Arriaga, Inglewood Police Department
Dave Avila, Los Angeles Police Department
David Avila Jr., Los Angeles Sheriff's Department
Mercy Avila, Los Angeles County DCFS
Albert and Millie Balderas
George Bernier, Los Angeles Police Department (retired)
Chris Blatchford, Fox 11 News, Los Angeles
Yolanda Bybee, Los Angeles Police Department
Wayne Caffey, Los Angeles Police Department
California Gang Investigators Association (CGIA)
California Gang Task Force (CGTF)
Jose Carrillo, Los Angeles Police Department
Michael Chettleburgh, Astwood Strategy Corporation
Cecilia Cleveland, Los Angeles Police Department
Dennis Conte, LAPD/LASD
Rick Cornwell
Wes Dailey, East Coast Gang Investigators Association
Michelle Diaz, Los Angeles Police Department
Bob Dinlocker, Los Angeles Police Department

Kenny Doyle , Ottawa Police Service
Leo Duarte, California Department of Corrections
Dave Enlow, Los Angeles Police Department (retired)
Dennis Fanning, Los Angeles Police Department
John Fletcher, Los Angeles Police Department
Gil Garcia, California Youth Authority
Paul Glascow, Los Angeles Police Department
Mike Grant, Los Angeles Police Department
Colleen Grosso, California Department of Corrections (retired)
Terry Hara, Los Angeles Police Department
Al Harden, Los Angeles Police Department (Rest in Peace)
Susie Harrison
 "Uncle Rick" Harrison, Ottawa-Carleton Reg. Detention Center
Joe Holmes, Los Angeles Sheriff's Department
Ed Hulbert, Los Angeles Police Department
International Latino Gang Investigators Association
Jerry Kaono, Los Angeles Sheriff's Department
Tom Layton, Los Angeles County Sheriff's Department
Pierre "Pedro" Lescadre, Royal Canadian Mounted Police
Los Angeles County Sheriff's Department – Sheriff Lee Baca
Los Angeles Police Department – Chief William Bratton
Los Angeles Police Protective League
Louise Logue, Ottawa Police Service
Shelly Lowe, New Jersey State Police
Natalie Macias, Los Angeles County Sheriff's Department
Manny Madrid Jr., Los Angeles Sheriff's Department
Manny Madrid Sr.   (Rest in Peace)
Wes McBride, LASD (retired), President of CGIA
Kevin McCarthy, Los Angeles Police Department
Al McGilvray, Los Angeles Police Department (Rest in Peace)
Jorge Martinez, Los Angeles Police Department
Josie Miller (Cortinas), Los Angeles Police Department
Tom Molinaro
Anthony Moreno
"Uncle Carlos" Moreno
"Dickie" Moreno, Los Angeles Sheriff's Department (retired)
Rose Moreno
"Big John" Munguia, Los Angeles Police Department (retired)
Dan Nalian, West Covina Police Department

New Jersey State Police – Superintendent Rick Fuentes
Sue O'Sullivan, Ottawa Police Service
Ottawa Police Service, Canada – Chief Vince Bevan
Brian Parry, California Department of Corrections (retired)
Nora Perez , Los Angeles County Probation
Mike Poirier, Los Angeles Sheriff's Department
Steve Polak, Los Angeles Police Department (retired)
Trinka Porrata, Los Angeles Police Department (retired)
Bourbon Quijano, Los Angeles Police Department
Ricky Ramos, Los Angeles Police Department
Jim "Rammer" Ramsay, Ottawa Police Service
John Ramsay
Mary Ridgeway, Los Angeles County Probation
Mario Rios, Los Angeles Police Department
Max Ross, Los Angeles Police Department
Bob Ruchhoft, Los Angeles Police Department (retired)
"Uncle Robert" Samario
Adam Smith
Charles "Ted" Spicer, Los Angeles Police Department
Joe Suarez, Los Angeles Police Department (retired)
Craig Taylor, Los Angeles Police Department
Mike Thompson, Los Angeles Police Department (retired)
Hugo Trujillo, Los Angeles Police Department
Raul Vega, Los Angeles Police Department
Dave Waterman, Los Angeles Police Department (retired)
Dave Wentworth , Los Angeles Police Department
Rob Wightman, Ontario Police Department, California
"Bubba" Williams, Los Angeles County Sheriff's Department
Paul Yablonsky, California Youth Authority (retired)
Chuck Zeglin, Los Angeles Police Department

About the Author

A 30-year veteran with the LAPD, Tony Moreno is a qualified gang specialist who has devoted his career to developing information on gangs, investigating gangs and gang-related crime, and providing training to thousands of law enforcement professionals, agencies and private companies. Tony's reputation as a gang cop is well chronicled. The nickname given to him by gang members, "Pacman", and the yellow Plymouth Fury police vehicle he drove for five years were used in the story line of the 1988 movie *Colors*, starring Robert Duvall and Sean Penn. For more information on Mr. Moreno's achievements, please visit his web site at www.gangcop.com. Email: tomoreno@hotmail.com